AF333777

*It Was a
Wonderful Summer
for
Running Away* ....

•••

Also by Charles N. Barnard

THE WINTER PEOPLE

20,000 ALARMS

I DRANK THE WATER EVERYWHERE

It Was a
Wonderful Summer
for
Running Away

CHARLES N. BARNARD

DODD, MEAD & COMPANY, NEW YORK

Library of Congress Cataloging in Publication Data

Barnard, Charles N
It was a wonderful summer for running away.

I. Title.
PZ4.B25867It   [PS3552.A6736]   813'.5'4   78–17282
ISBN 0–396–07574–6

For Peter Weed
who said this might be done
and for Karen
who said I should try

.... *Foreword*

Some of this happened, some of it did not.

Some of the people are real, they lived. Some are real enough even if they did not.

Nineteen thirty six was what some people now call the good old days. It was when things were still built-like-they-used-to-be. Despite the depression, we had nothing to fear but fear, we were told. There was peace in the world, we thought, and no trouble at home because everybody knew his place.

But there was no joy either; joy was out of fashion. We only enjoyed the questionable nobility of being poor and surviving.

c.n.b.

1

OVERNIGHT, my world had taken a new tilt. It wasn't just the picture on the Currier and Ives calendar that had been turned over. An earth signal was being transmitted and received. My mother had opened one of the kitchen windows for the first time since winter. Puffs of sweet April air entered like whispered invitations from resurrected spirits. Come outside! said Spirit of Green Grass. Take off your shirt! said Spirit of Warm Sunshine. Get ready! said Spirit of Summer Coming.

It was the Saturday spring arrived.

I ate my breakfast dutifully, distracted from food by the scents and suggestions that were seeping into the room. I chewed the prunes and *expectorated* the pits properly into my spoon. I finished all the porridge without mentioning the lumps (pressing them out with my tongue against the roof of my mouth). Nothing—no unfinished portion of food, no complaint, no lapse of table manners ("You're sitting on your napkin again, Charles!")—nothing must interfere with my freedom to escape the house this day.

I downed the last swallow of milk, charged upstairs to brush my teeth with baking soda and comb my hair, then presented myself in the kitchen again, a candidate for parole, winter's prisoner wanting out.

"Don't go too far." It was what my mother always said.

"I won't," I answered, just as I always did.

I ran from my mother, ran from the house, counting to see how many strides I could take across the lawn before I heard the storm door slam behind me.

One, two (past the well), *three, four—bang!* went the old spring-powered door. Someday I'd make it to *five,* make it all the way to the lilac hedge before I heard the pistol shot at my back.

Beyond the budding lilacs, last year's wild grass was still brown and dry in the fields and laced with blackberry vines that grabbed at my pants as I ran, tugging for an instant, then ripping loose, leaving tiny rows of thorns stitched into brown corduroy. I imagined jungle vines and felt myself slashing through them with a machete in tropical heat. You can't hold me! I cried, I'm escaping, I'm free!

And I was. School was over for the week (and almost for the year), Saturday breakfast and its rituals were done, the storm door had fired its shot and missed me again. I remember it all not because it happened that way so often, but because it happened that way only once.

The day this particular spring arrived was the beginning of a special year.

Along a tumbled stone wall that marked a forgotten boundary south of the house, a cluster of young cedars had spread out and grown up around a strong-armed old tree that still stood tallest in the group. Greenbriar had taken hold and climbed into some of the other trees, hanging in thorny curtains, as if nature wished to close this dark little grove to intruders.

I knew how to reach the interior without getting a scratch or disturbing a branch. It was my secret hideout, at least one of them. I had others too. The wagon path, the railroad station, Airplane Pond. But when I was in the cedar grove, I had a special sort of privacy. I could look out across the fields and see my house clearly, even make out my mother's silhouette behind the kitchen windows, but I knew she couldn't see me or even guess my whereabouts. Like a hunter, I was hidden in a blind. Or, was I the one hunted? Whenever I stayed away too long, Mother would go to the back door and ring the old brass sleigh bell—I was supposed to come home at once. I always did, too, always had, ever since I was a little boy, but now I didn't like to hear the bell any more, didn't like to have it follow me through the air and enter the cedar grove and reach inside my head and make me automatically do something.

That's what don't-go-too-far was all about. It was the range of the sleigh bell, the maximum reach of Mother's authority.

The deeply shaded chamber enclosed by the cedars was as clear of dead limbs or branches as if pruned by tree surgeons. Shaped like a Gothic arch it reached high into the oldest, biggest tree. The air in this space seemed as still as in a church even when there was a breeze outside; and if the sun was hot in the fields, here it was always cool. Light filtered through the dark branches, flashing in my eyes like sequins when I looked up.

On the ground a deep cinnamon-colored carpet yielded softly and made no sound when I walked on it. It was like a well-raked path in a public park, but unmarred by any footprints, dusted with soft brown siftings that fell silently from the branches above.

I had come to this place as long as I could remember, at

least since I was eight or nine. I enjoyed the excitement of hiding here, of seeing but not being seen.

I also liked to watch the red ants that lived under the trees. They used the soft, bran-brown cedar mulch to build their mounds. There were three mounds, bigger than any ant hills I had ever seen in the Territory around my house. They stood almost two feet above ground and were nearly three feet across. They could have been mistaken for piles of dirt and sometimes I thought they looked like a miniature native village in Africa, the kind of round, bowl-shaped houses that the Masai built with mud and dung. I had seen such pictures in *National Geographic.*

Listen. Hear the drums? *I* heard them.

I found a book about insects at the library and learned that ant colonies of this size might have a population of hundreds of thousands. The book also said that red ants were meat eaters, that when they found an animal carcass, they picked it surgically clean, often leaving a perfect skeleton. There was something quite frightening about that.

When I first discovered the ants, I was satisfied to just sit on the ground near one of the mounds and watch scouting parties with a magnifying glass. Looking at them this way, I observed that the ants were rusty red in color, quick moving, nervous, alert, nothing like the lumbering black ants I used to find in rotted wood. Black ants never seemed to go far from their nests, but red ants were adventurers. They were intelligent too. I was sure they were able to see, hear and understand. A sound or vibration would make them stop in their tracks, trembling with alarm. A thump on the ground would bring them up on their hind legs, front feet and antennae pawing to locate the danger.

They were like an army, I thought, armored columns on maneuvers, a horde, an enemy force. Or were they my

4

friends? I knew they could bite, as I had been stung a few times when one of their stray scouts was caught between my shoe and sock and had to fight his way out. The bite was painful. In retribution, I would bombard the ants with small, dry balls of yellow clay which, when they landed, burst like World War I shells over No Man's Land. *Wheeeeooooh, boom!* Then the ants would stop and quiver and regroup their battalions.

I had watched the ants from one year to another; I felt an old companionship with them. Sometimes, in winter, I would think about them and wonder how they were surviving the snow and cold. When the earth thawed each year, I waited for their first appearance.

In this spring of 1936, because of world events and the nightly news broadcasts of Lowell Thomas, my ants became the German Army. They were, I could plainly see, getting ready for war. As everyone knew, the German ants were marvelously disciplined and probably unbeatable. Other ants would be no match for them. On maneuvers, I watched their pincer movements sweep across France. From my own strongpoint in the Maginot Line, I kept my glasses trained on their mobilizations. It would have been easy to lob a heavy mortar shell into their midst, causing horrible carnage, but that would surely have provoked an incident with Hitler. I knew the world wasn't ready for that.

"Where have you been playing?" my mother asked when I returned to the house for lunch. I hated the term "playing." Little kids *played!* Now that I was fourteen and grown up, Mother didn't seem to notice that I no longer *played.* I went out of the house, did things, and came back.

She didn't understand my maturity. She didn't understand ants either. She sprayed them.

2

I REMEMBER 1936 as special because that was the year I decided to run away. I'll never forget the whole crazy business. It lasted all summer and went through stages, like a head cold. Making the plans occupied me day after day; week after week, which was just as well because there wasn't much else to do.

It was only a notion at first, the kind of dreamy scheme youngsters put together in their heads but never do anything about, not really. Then it somehow became real and pretty soon it seemed I had started something I couldn't stop and might *have* to run away whether I wanted to or not.

I dreamed up this idea all by myself, without any encouragement from anyone and with no one to share my huge secret. That was a trouble about 1936, at least where I lived. There just weren't as many *people* as there are today and the ones we had were mostly old and worried about being poor and didn't have time for kids with silly ideas.

There was definitely a shortage of boys in 1936 too. Artie Wiggin was about the only one in my neighborhood and he could be strange. Sometimes he kept a wad of bacon and peanut butter in his mouth half the morning. Every once in a while he'd chew it a little, then tongue it back into his cheek like a chaw of tobacco. He said it kept him from getting too hungry before lunch.

I was my widowed mother's only child. We lived in a big old house on a country road, about a mile from the center of a small town that I hated. Hancock, Massachusetts, was not necessarily worse than other towns, I suppose, but that didn't matter. I told myself that I hated them all.

Anything of importance in Hancock was built of brick. Along Uptown's main street, called Main Street, there was a red brick bank, a red brick post office and a red brick "business block" that housed two drugstores, a hardware store, an auto supply and a J. J. Newberry's 5 & 10¢. There was also a small diner called the Lunch Cart.

Beyond the red brick railroad station were the red brick textile mills, long three-story buildings with countless windows and tall chimneys from which no smoke or steam arose in 1936. There was also the boarded-up remains of the Globe theatre, the only place around to see a movie until it burned down one night.

Seemingly untouched by economic disaster was the red brick Academy where my mother said I must go to school. The main building looked a little like a church, and was surrounded by playing fields, tennis courts, blue spruce trees, elms and green acres. Also immune to the Depression was the town library, built of granite with heavy bronze doors like a bank. We had several churches, most of them white clapboard except for the Catholic church, which was red brick.

On the elm-shaded Common was a bandstand and a World War I memorial statue of a doughboy holding his helmet in his hands, head bowed. Some nice old private homes stood near the center of town, big rambling houses with broad porches and cupolas on top. In 1936, many needed painting.

The small, uncomplicated layout of the town's business and residential areas could be learned in a day. As the various streets wandered off into the surrounding farmland, most just turned into country roads. I lived on the one called Maple Street. It was blacktop almost all the way to where the street lights stopped.

I don't really know how the idea to run away got started. No one I knew had ever done it, unless it was true that the Wendell girl, who also lived on my street, had run away the year before and had a baby when she was fifteen. I always supposed that people ran away when conditions at home became "intolerable." I can't remember exactly what I was thinking, but suddenly there were many reasons for running away, all of them good, all of them perfectly logical.

Sometimes, as the idea developed, I wrote them down, 1, 2, 3. Then I had a *set* of reasons for running away, a complete set. Looking at the list was reassuring.

When the dirigible *Hindenburg* crossed the Atlantic in 1936, I was prompted to announce that *I* yearned to fly too. I was tall enough now to see beyond my home town, I said, and would not be satisfied to just stand on a barn roof and look over the next pasture like some people around here. (I never actually stood on a barn roof, but it was a neat figure of speech, I thought). After all, I brooded, Mussolini was conquering Ethiopia, Germany was escaping from its borders and Alvin Karpis was leading J. Edgar Hoover a merry chase. Everybody was busting out; it was in the air. So why not me?

Of course, we had no television in 1936, so I had not really seen any of these important events unfolding, but we had *Life* magazine and Lowell Thomas on the radio every night at 6:45 and the *American Weekly* on Sundays and movie magazines and rotogravure and newsreels. You didn't have to look very far to see that there were more exciting places than Hancock.

The Depression was also a big part of my problem. By 1936, it had depressed everything. Sometimes I thought the Depression must have begun right in my town, somewhere between the shutdown woolen mills that had put everybody out of work and the burned-down movie theatre the owners said they couldn't afford to rebuild. The Depression was an accident that had first happened right here, a match that had been dropped, and then spread out to the rest of the country. But *we* were at the center, so it couldn't possibly be any worse than right where I lived.

Then, of course, my mother was a reason for running away too. That was natural. Parents were always one of the things kids ran away from. My mother meant well, but most of the time I didn't understand her and I was positive she didn't understand me at all. Sometimes she said she didn't give a hoot for Hancock either, only lived in the town because she had to. She made this sound as though she had been planted in this certain location long ago and now it was too late to do anything about it. But sometimes she defended the place too, which was odd because my mother's favorite claim to social distinction was the fact that she'd "seen the world," she'd traveled, she'd ridden on camels here and rickshaws there, she said—and she had taken me with her. I didn't remember as much about these travels as she wished I would, especially when she wanted me to impress grownups by telling them how much I loved Paris.

(Actually, the only thing I could recall about Paris, besides drinking some pink-colored stuff at sidewalk cafes, was the big fight I had with a four-year-old French kid who threw sand at me in a park, followed by the big fight my mother had with the boy's mother, each of them holding onto her own offspring and screaming at the other in two languages. It was all very exciting as far as I was concerned and definitely the highpoint of my visit to Paris, France.)

Mother's travels always seemed to be with us, even on Maple Street. For example, she had an embroidered shawl that was a souvenir of Spain. She said it was very valuable. It was faded black silk with a slightly tangled fringe and she kept it in a Jordan Marsh box in the attic, but once in a while Mother would get it out and spin it around her shoulders and tell me not to worry, that if the Depression got real bad, she'd sell the Spanish Shawl.

Well, anyway, in the spring of 1936 I began making plans to run away. Summer was coming and school would be out and that would be the best time. Summer was the season of possibilities. Winter, on the other hand, shriveled me. I would never have thought about running anywhere in winter. Cold occupied my Territory then and stiffened the honey of my imagination. That was my phrase for it.

But summer didn't require shelter or a hot stove for comfort. Summer was earthy warmth, summer was freedom again. Summer always made me feel the way I wanted to feel: like my own self. And the summer of 1936 seemed as if it were the first time I looked far away and smiled at the distant temptations I thought I saw.

3

Artie Wiggin twisted his hands around the handle
of the bat until his two brown fists seemed to be wringing its
neck. Then he crouched over home plate—the end cut out
of an orange crate—and held the bat cocked behind his right
shoulder. Artie's arms were so long they made the bat look
short.

"What you want?" I asked, hiding the baseball behind my
back and leaning in toward the batter. "Fast ball or curve?"

"Jes throw it, I'll hit it."

I thought of myself as a control pitcher. I was also working
on my submarine ball. Actually, I hoped Artie would hit
whatever I threw because there was no catcher. I also hoped
he wouldn't hit it too far because there were no outfielders.
There were just the two of us.

I threw hard, trying to hold my fingers in a certain way
on the stitches. The ball sailed high and outside. Artie un-
coiled his long linkage of arms and bat and whacked an
arching fly down the right field line.

"Foul ball!"

"Nah, fair!" Artie said, standing his ground at the plate.
In our game, the batter was supposed to recover his own
fouls, the pitcher had to shag anything that fell fair. The right

field foul pole in my yard was an elm tree on the lawn. The ball had dropped fair.

Artie Wiggin was my best friend in some ways, considering I didn't have much choice. He was nothing like a brother, but he was the only boy in the neighborhood close to my age and we got along okay except that sometimes Artie seemed a little stupid. Like that peanut butter and bacon business.

Actually, Artie didn't have much free time either. His father worked him so hard on the hen farm he barely had time to play baseball in the afternoons when spring came. Whenever he did, he'd just come trudging through the fields between our houses bringing his baseball and glove and maybe a dozen eggs my mother had ordered from his father. Mother always said that Mr. Wiggin's eggs were good, "no fishy taste at all."

"I'll give him that much," she'd say, "his eggs are good, no fishy taste at all. Not like the Armenian's eggs," she'd go on. "Armenians will feed anything to their hens."

I didn't know how Mother knew so much about so many people, except perhaps as a result of her travels. Anyway, I gathered that it must be a misfortune to be an Armenian.

I was fourteen, Artie Wiggin was fifteen and big for his age. He had the longest arms I'd ever seen. I wondered if they got that way from farm work. They hung down the sides of his body like they'd been permanently stretched from carrying heavy loads; and his big, brown hands waggled at the ends of his wrists as though somehow loosened from being too far from the rest of him.

Artie was comic in a somber sort of way. Everything about him seemed elongated. He had a long, sober expression to go with his long arms and wore long bib overalls the same size as his father's. Sometimes he smelled of disinfectant and there was always chicken manure wedged in the space between the soles and heels of his shoes. His hair was usually clipped so short that his scalp showed white on the side.

I think if I had put the question to him, straight out: Artie, are you my friend? he would have smiled but squinched his blue eyes tight shut. That was always his way of saying let's change the subject.

I knew if I asked him if he'd ever thought about running away, he'd probably squinch his eyes and keep them shut until I said something else.

All the same, Artie was the only person I could think of who might make a running away partner. Someday, I was going to find out how he might feel about leaving his father's hen farm for good. I didn't see why he wouldn't want to.

I had had the idea from the beginning that it would be easier and more fun if I didn't run away alone, if I could do it with a pal, the way it usually happened in stories. Of course, this meant I would have to find someone who wanted to run away as badly as I did. There must be other kids in this category. I usually pictured a friend who was my age: fourteen. He would be just like me in most ways, maybe like a brother. I wasn't sure about this because I didn't have a real brother, just a make-believe brother who was a little older than I, had blond hair, and was an expert pistol shot. He also had a pretty girl friend and was learning to fly a Piper Cub.

I knew for sure I wouldn't find my running away partner at the Academy. The Boarding Students there came from all over the country, or at least all over New England and New York. That was the problem. Because these kids all lived somewhere else already, they didn't have to run away like I did.

Day students and boarding students were two very different categories. I lived with my mother on Maple Street and walked up the road to classes every day. There were only a few of us in this category. We had our own separate locker room with a sink that sat in the corner with its faucets perpetually dripping, like an admonition from the school authorities to wash our hands before joining the rest of the student body.

Boarding students lived upstairs in the dormitories. They had nice rooms with big high windows and soft, woolen blankets neatly folded at the foot of their beds and college pennants pinned to the walls. Boarding students came from places like Rye, New York, and had tweed overcoats to wear on Sunday and they called day students "day hops."

There were girls at the Academy too. Girl boarding students. They lived in one wing of the school and boys in the other and there was always gossip in Hancock about how the Academy boys and girls got together at night after the lights were out, like rabbits. Mother heard these stories from her friends and believed them. As a consequence, she was always warning me to stay away from the Academy girls. She didn't seem to understand that whatever Academy girls might do after the lights were out, they didn't do it with day hops.

After I ran away, I told myself, I wouldn't be a Day Hop any more. Or an Only Child, either. And I hoped that somewhere I would find girls who didn't come from Rye, New York, and wouldn't talk all the time about going dancing at a place called the Glen Island Casino, whatever was so great about that.

"Do you *like* going to the Academy?" Artie asked me one day.

"It's all right." I couldn't tell Artie I didn't like it.

Most town kids thought it was really something to go to the Academy, although they wouldn't say so. If Artie thought it was something great, I wasn't going to argue with him. Usually, town boys and girls didn't have much to do with anybody who went to the Academy anyway, not even day hops.

"Any of them Academy girls ever get pregnant?" Artie asked.

Because the Academy was coeducational, with both sexes living under one roof, this seemed to excite the imagination of most of Hancock.

"Nah, not a chance," I said.

"How come? Why not? They old enough, ain't they?" Artie guffawed like Mortimer Snerd.

"You're crazy, Artie. There's no way it could happen."

"I hear it can happen lots of ways. I hear there's a place 'way up in the steeple where they go."

"Not a chance! They got bed checks and everything."

"Wendell girl got pregnant."

"What's that got to do with it? She doesn't go to the Academy." I had heard the rumor about the Wendell girl before.

Artie grinned slyly.

The Wendell girl was the only other public school student who lived in my neighborhood. She must have been almost sixteen, I thought, and she was sexy in a way, even if you didn't know the stories about her having the baby. Of course she wasn't sexy like Jean Harlow, my favorite actress, but her face was pretty. She had dark hair and nice legs and a good smile, except for a cavity between her two front teeth. She lived with her mother and father and two older brothers in a small farm house that had been occupied by several different families just in my memory. They had all been renters, people who moved in and out. I guess the Wendells were renters too. Mother said renters were cheap trash, all of them, not the sort of people who used to live on our street in the old days.

Renters and Armenians were pretty much the same in Mother's view.

It was true, the Wendell house was no model of neatness. Old cars were parked on what had once been a front lawn, sometimes two or three of them, each occupying its own well-worn oily spot. Mr. Wendell and his two sons worked at the tap and die factory while Mrs. Wendell must have spent a lot of time doing wash because there was always a long flapping string of clothes hanging on the line.

I'd said hello to the Wendell girl a few times when we'd passed on the road, but except for that, we didn't really know each other because she was older and went to high school already. Also, who knows? Maybe she had been a mother too, which, if it was a fact, aged her considerably in my view.

Sometimes I used to see town boys giving the Wendell girl a ride home in their cars. They would park on one of the vacant oily spots on the Wendell front lawn. They would, that is, until Mrs. Wendell came to the door and sent them away. Mrs. Wendell had quite a vocabulary when she wanted to get rid of boys.

Actually, I wasn't sure of the Wendell girl's first name, but I thought I'd heard her called Roxy by her brothers. Even though she was a neighbor, I had the same problem about her that I had with Academy girls. I didn't know how to make conversation with them and I especially didn't know how to talk to the Wendell girl. She wouldn't be interested in baseball or Mussolini or ants or the *Hindenburg,* I didn't think. She smelled of perfume. And she always wore a black brassiere that I could see through her blouse.

So that was the situation between me and the Wendell girl when we happened to meet one day after school; and there wasn't any way to get out of walking down Maple Street together since we were both headed in the same direction at the same time. We started talking about nothing in particular, but after a couple of minutes I relaxed because she seemed friendly enough and even somewhat interested to know more about me. For instance, she asked me how long I had been going to the Academy and I told her this was my second year, but I was really still in eighth grade because the Academy was the same as junior high and high school together.

"You going to college, too?" she asked. I said yes, I hoped so because college would mean being able to go away and that's what I most wanted.

"I hear you've been just about everywhere in the world," she said. "Is that true?"

I told her my mother had toured all over Europe and other places after Father died, but that I didn't remember much about it. I didn't like to talk about our travels. They weren't my travels, they were Mother's Travels. She was the one always mentioning them and showing people the Spanish shawl and everything.

We were almost at the Wendell girl's house when I finally got up the courage to ask, "Is your name really Roxy?"

She looked at me as if I had discovered some awful secret. "I hate that," she said. "It sounds like a movie house. They named me Roxanne, but I'd rather be called Annie."

She was turning off the road now, walking through the weeds, taking a shortcut that led into her side yard.

"Okay," I said, feeling much better about things, "nice talking to you, Annie." She didn't turn her head again, she just kept going toward the house. When she was halfway across the yard, she waved one hand over her head without turning around and said, "So long, Chuck."

Nobody ever called me Chuck, but I liked it anyway.

Annie Wendell left the scent of her perfume behind even after she was out of sight. She was much nicer than I had thought. Maybe I'd get to know her better this summer. The idea filled me with a strange nervousness.

I wondered if it was true that she'd had a kid already.

●●●●●●●●●●●●●●●●●● *4*

MY house, the big colonial-style box where I lived with Mother, never seemed to be mine, not really mine, not a place where I could tack a *National Geographic* map of Africa to the wall of my room without wondering if I might be causing pain to some ancestor whose spirit still resided in the old pig-bristle plaster, someone who might still be looking after things, someone like my father's Aunt Maria, whose presence I always felt most keenly. My room had once been hers, I was told. There was a small cupboard over the fireplace where she had kept her books and a china tea set and many, many pairs of gloves, all styles and colors.

"She was a little crazy," Mother used to say. "She spent most of her time right in this room."

I imagined an eccentric old lady, hobbling around.

"Toward the end, she kept saying that some day she was going to run away. She must have thought she was a child again."

"And did she ever?"

"Run away? Of course not. She died right here, right where your bed is now."

Other rooms in the house also had histories. There were many rooms and many stories. Actually, the place was 'way

19

too big for us, but Mother always said The Estate had to be preserved. It had been my father's and his father's and *his* father's, I guess, and keeping it all untouched seemed to be some sort of obligation to posterity.

The Estate consisted of a main house, a garage converted from a horse barn and fourteen acres of land that had once been pasture, but had now pretty much grown up to a tangle of young cedars and pines, blueberry bushes, wild cherry, sumac scrub and blackberry vines.

The house was built in 1792, there was a door knocker with a date to prove it. The barn—or at least its foundations—was supposed to be older, going all the way back to 1640. Neither structure looked authentically old in 1936, however, because of a 1920s remodeling that removed the original white clapboard exterior and multi-pane windows, also various woodsheds, well houses, privies, pantries, ovens and closets. The house was now clad in a sand-colored cement stucco with brick porches and fieldstone pillars supporting a *porte-cochère,* which Mother called the porta-shay.

All this sat very close to the edge of the road, looking as if it had been armor plated by some previous occupant fearing an attack.

The house seemed huge to me when I was small. Mother contributed to this image by always speaking of its great size—and expense. "Fifty-two windows and seven exterior doors!" she would say. Then she'd add that she wished we didn't have to keep such a place, not just the two of us. But keep it, apparently, we must.

It was always *we* where the house was concerned, as if I had something to do with the problem because I was my father's son. I didn't really think I should be blamed for having a father who didn't live long enough.

20

Mother wasn't always complaining. Sometimes she seemed to accept the burden of Father's estate as a noble responsibility. It was a symbol of family continuity, she said. Like the Parthenon. Mother had seen the Parthenon in her travels in Greece. She had also seen a lot of piazzas in Italy, so she called the brick porch around the house the pee-azza.

Airs is what the old lady across the street called this. "Your ma's got airs," she'd say to me. Once when she said this, Ada swiveled her big old backside halfway around and through her lips made the sound of breaking wind. "That's what your ma's full of!" she said with a mischievous smile. "Airs." Ada was a funny, wrinkled old woman and I loved her. I suspected she was right about my mother, but didn't let on that I agreed. Our house didn't have fifty-two windows or seven exterior doors, not even if you counted the attic and the cellar; but I never corrected Mother about anything. I never called the pee-azza the porch. And I never asked Mother how she got to be a stock market broker either, although I wondered about that sometimes. It seemed an unusual thing for a woman to do, especially in sleepy old Hancock.

Besides the house, which never seemed to be mine, I didn't have a family either, not in the usual, Mom-and-Pop, Brothers-and-Sisters sense. I had what Mother called a "distinguished lineage." And, worse, I was one of those creatures called an Only Child. It was a category. My mother was a category too—actually, she was several. One was Only Mother. "I'm your only mother," she would say, "the only one you'll ever have." Categories created conditions of life that had to be accepted, it appeared. I understood that there was no intended discrimination in this, just bad luck. You could get to be an only child in a number of ways, none of them disgraceful, but all of them somehow regrettable, I thought.

Mother used to say that if my father had lived, I wouldn't have amounted to a hill of beans. A hill of beans was one of her favorite expressions, but I could never picture it. Were they baked beans or green beans? Nevertheless, I made no smart answers about how I might have had a brother if Father had lived.

My mother also said that my father would have spoiled me rotten with all those fancy guns and cars of his. I didn't make any snappy answers about that either, but my father's luxuries always sounded like wonderful ways to be a failure in life. What was wrong with fancy guns and cars? I wished some of them were still around, but they left with Father.

Sometimes, when Mother talked to other people about my father, she would tell them how he went to Detroit every year to select his new Cadillac at the factory. Of course, when she talked to others about Father's way of life, she didn't make it sound like extravagance at all, just the kind of thing any wealthy man might do. I imagined his long, cross-country trips to Detroit and wished I could have made one with him. No one went to Detroit to pick out a car any more but maybe after the Depression was over, it could be done again—if you told Cadillac you were coming.

I remembered every fact and story I'd ever been told about my father. I knew how tall he was, how much he weighed, and how fine his hair was (like mine) and how he wore gold cufflinks and used to race his own horses at the Brockton Fair. I knew all about the trap shooting and the trophies he won at the Boston Athletic Association—and I knew the room in which he died. There was a place on the mahogany headboard of his bed where the finish was roughened, a place where he had laid back his head after an alcohol rub, Mother said, leaving the imprint of his hair as clear in 1936 as when he had been alive in 1921.

I always had trouble picturing Father's face because we had only two old sepia photos of him. Whenever I thought about leaving home, I told myself I wasn't going to be running away from him. I was going to take him with me.

The more I thought about running away, the more it turned into a category all its own: Running Away. I told myself it wasn't really such a terrible thing I was thinking of doing. It was traditional, wasn't it? Even Aunt Maria had talked about it. Kids were always running away in books, weren't they? I'd read lots of stories describing the procedure. They put some food and a compass and some other stuff into a handkerchief and tied it to the end of a stick, then left home and headed toward trains and hobo jungles.

When I was younger, there had been a bedtime story that Mother used to tell me about a little boy who ran away. I must have liked it because I could remember asking for it. Tell me the story of the little boy who ran away, I could hear myself saying; and the memory made me cringe.

"Well, once there was the little boy who decided to run away from home . . ." She always told it as if running away only happened in stories.

"How old was he?" (How old do you have to be? I wondered.)

"About the same as you."

"Why did he run away?"

"He was bad."

"Didn't his mother love him?"

"Oh, of course she did! Mothers always love their children. But this little boy was very bad."

"Go on."

"So he put all his things in a little suitcase and then he ran off up the road from his nice big house where his mother was and by nightfall he was far away in the woods, all by himself, and he was cold and hungry."

"Did anyone find him?" (Of course, they did. They always did.)

"Now you know the story as well as I do," my mother would say. "Why don't you tell the rest of it?"

And then I'd finish the story and explain how homesick the little boy became and how he missed the nice supper that his mother always fixed. (The little boy in this story didn't seem to have a father either.)

"You wouldn't ever run away like that, would you?"

"No, Mother."

This brief catechism was an official part of the story. It came just before the instruction, Go-to-sleep-now.

My room in the house was upstairs on the southwest corner. From the two windows I could see the cedar grove and our garage and a piece of Artie Wiggin's henhouse, also the brick tower of the Catholic Church on the horizon, Uptown. There was a big, round, braided rug on the floor that Mother had made from old cut-up strips of horse blankets. I also had a white iron bed, a dark mahogany dresser with an oval mirror mounted on it, two hard, cane-seat chairs on which I never sat and a yellow oak desk Mother said was old and should be called a Secretary Desk. It had a bottom drawer that could be locked with a brass key. In this drawer I kept an assortment of miscellaneous treasures and necessities: a pen flashlight I snitched from the dime store because I thought I'd need it; a magnifying glass that, under the summer sun, was strong enough to start a fire in dry grass; a compass in a brass case; a blob of liquid mercury from a broken thermometer; a pearl-handled pocket knife that had been Father's; several spent shotgun shells; assorted Tom Mix Club paraphernalia, including the secret code book; several pictures of Jean Harlow, clipped from the *American Weekly*; the Lionel train catalogs for 1934 and 1935; my father's waterproof container for matches; a buckskin leather wallet bought on top of Mt. Washington in New Hampshire (no money in it); a red silk handkerchief that belonged with my magic tricks; a collection of gum cards depicting Indian chiefs; a Big Little Book about heavyweight champion Joe Louis; all the parts to make a scale model Weeden steam engine; a holy medal Mother said had been blessed by the Pope in Rome (we weren't Catholic); the gear mechanism from an old clock; a Tootsietoy race car made to look like Sir Malcolm Campbell's Bluebird; a nickle-plated Hubley cap pistol called the G-Man Special; some razor clam shells from our trip to Cape Cod; several birthday and Hallowe'en cards; a crumble of wax crayons; some antique spark plugs from my father's early Cadillacs; a dentist's plaster impression of my front teeth (which were crooked but weren't going to get straightened because of the Depression); the license tags from Father's last hunting dog, a setter named Flossie; a piece of crushed aircraft aluminum dug up from the place in the woods where the Army plane had crashed; a blue and white Hoover button; a green Conklin fountain pen with a real gold tip and a dried up rubber bladder inside; a glass tiddledywinks cup full of Indian head pennies; the unfinished fuselage of a Fokker tri-plane carved from a block of balsa wood; a deck of playing cards with a picture of the Moxie man on their backs; a cricket clicker bearing the name of a shore dinner restaurant in Rocky Point, Rhode Island; and, in a small notebook, a list of the fireworks I bought last Fourth of July.

In the same notebook I wrote down a list of my reasons for running away. It read:

1) Because nothing ever happens here

2) Because I want to do some of the things I would have done with Father

3) Because if I stay here, I'll get like Artie Wiggin

4) Because I don't want to go back to the Academy again next year

5) Because I'll never grow up as long as I'm here where everybody thinks I'm just a kid.

$$\cdots\cdots\cdots\cdots\cdots\; 5$$

"ACROSS-THE-STREET" was Mother's name for the small farm house that stood on the other side of the road from her own fifty-two-windows-and-seven-doors. The term also applied to the two old people who lived in the house; Mother seemed to prefer calling them simply and collectively, Across-the-street, than by their names.

Ada McMillan was in her eighties, her son George in his sixties. They weren't farmers. At some long-ago time they had both worked in the old factories in New York state and Connecticut where hats were made from fur felt. When that trade died out, they settled on the small, one-time farm across from us. Their hearts weren't in farming, however, and their ages were against them. By 1936, fighting off poverty was their main occupation, but they were uncomplaining.

"Across-the-street thinks we've got all kinds of money because I'm a professional woman and we keep this big house," Mother would say, or "Across-the-street doesn't appreciate what our Estate does for the neighborhood." Sometimes she said, "Across-the-street wouldn't lift a finger to help if I was dying alone in this big house." The fact that she was neither dying nor alone made me wonder what she really meant.

In spite of Mother's prejudices, or more likely because of them, I liked to visit Across-the-street. From the earliest time that I could remember, Ada McMillan had been like a kindly grandmother to me. It was Ada who had introduced me to the pleasures of a raw frankfurter as a tasty mid-morning snack. It was Ada who taught me how to straighten a bent nail or darn holes in screenwire or sharpen a scythe blade. Ada made piccalilli and jelly and wonderful pies, without consulting a recipe, and she could cut window glass or bust up the root system of the rhubarb patch with a crowbar once a year or predict the weather from the changing color of the barn roof. To me, she was both formidable and admirable.

Although George must have been twenty years younger than his mother, he might have been the same age as far as appearances went. Both of them were wrinkled, gray people with thin hair, false teeth and eyes in which the whites had turned the same color as the insides of grapes. They could have been taken for husband and wife instead of mother and son. In fact, they nattered at each other so much that I sometimes thought of them as an old married couple.

George was the only man in the territory who remotely resembled what my father had been called: a sportsman. This was another reason I liked to hang around Across-the-street. George had a shotgun and a rifle and fishing equipment and lots of box and spring traps. He trapped skunks in the fall, rendered their fat to make a waxy, white liniment for home use, then stretched and dried the hides inside out on thin, hand-shaped boards. Before Christmas, he sent these off to a company in Chicago that paid him 50 cents a pelt.

Sometimes George had three or four skins hanging up in the barn at the same time. I thought he must be a pretty good trapper. And I think George was flattered by my attention to his outdoor skills because he was always showing me just how he did certain things, like setting the bait in a trap, or covering the jaws, or how to use the various scents and lures he kept in a row of old medicine bottles on a windowsill in the barn.

When I was ten or eleven, my obvious affection for Across-the-street and all the hours I spent visiting in the little yellow house didn't seem to trouble Mother much, but as I grew older, she treated my relationship with the two old people as something like a betrayal of class.

"I don't want to forbid you, understand, but I don't like you going over there so much," she would say. "It's not a fit household for a young man from a family like ours."

The unsuitability of Across-the-street for a teenage son of class was, in my mother's view, based on several facts. For one thing, Ada and George were, to be sure, provincials. "They've never been anywhere in their lives and they don't know the first thing about the world," she would say. This wasn't exactly true. I knew that both Ada and George had been to New York City many times in the old days, but I didn't want to argue.

Having applied her favorite yardstick of respectability to Across-the-street, Mother would go on to other things she didn't like about my friends. For instance, George *drank*. He swore, too, his favorite epithet being *By-jeez-Christ*! Further, Ada smoked even more cigarettes than George and she always answered the telephone by snapping "What-do-you-want?" into the receiver before she even knew who was calling.

In the spring of 1936, if there was anybody that I might have confided in about running away it would have probably been Ada and George. In my private, silent thoughts, I always took sides with them against my mother's views and I think they both knew this although we never talked about it. I was sure they would understand why I'd like to leave home if I could and I thought they might even be willing to help me.

For many years as I was growing up, Across-the-street always saved the Sunday comics from the Hearst paper for me. After a time, beginning when I was about twelve, I think, Ada also tucked in the *American Weekly* Sunday supplement, which was lurid enough in those innocent times to interest any kid. I especially liked the stories about the adventures of John Dillinger and Pretty Boy Floyd because such subjects were never discussed at home; nor was I ever allowed to see what were called "gangster movies."

Also in the *American Weekly,* pictures of Jean Harlow, braless in a white evening dress, or Dorothy Lamour in a sarong, warranted a certain amount of unblinking attention. Unhappily for my leisure reading and worldly education, Mother would not allow the *American Weekly* to cross the boundary of the family property, so I had to consume it, like the raw franks and cold pie, Across-the-street.

Inside, Across-the-street was always clean and tidy, although a little threadbare. The floors were uneven and the linoleum was nailed down and cracked. There was an iron cookstove with heat-warped lids in the kitchen, an oaken ice box with brass hinges and handles in the pantry, a tall, black stove that looked like a cemetery monument in the parlor, some odd pieces of old farm furniture here and there and two rocking chairs in which George and Ada usually sat facing each other in the evenings. A Stromberg-Carlson radio was placed on a small table between them with an aerial wire running out the nearest window. The radio had come into the house with Roosevelt's first election in 1932, but it was turned on only for important events, such as Admiral Byrd's broadcasts from Little America or the Fireside Chats—and sometimes in the morning for farm price reports. Even though George's farm never produced so much as a case of eggs or a bushel of pears for sale, it was still part of his daily ritual to know "what things should fetch," as he put it.

I couldn't get the two old people to listen to Jack Benny or Edgar Bergen or Ben Bernie or Joe Penner. The whole idea of comedians seemed to be lost on them. They seldom laughed at anything.

The barn, with its sagging roof, was directly behind the house. One side had been turned into a garage to accommodate an old Chevrolet two-door sedan, bottle green, with a leaky black top. The other side housed the Jersey cow named Buttercup, a couple of mean old rabbits that had been imprisoned for years in cages (and which George kept promising to eat one day), some banty roosters and a few hens. The barn was George's domain. He had a one-hole toilet near the cow stall. Even on winter mornings, he preferred this to the "flush commode" indoors.

George also had innumerable places here and there among the beams and joists of the barn where he concealed his pints and half pints of Seagram's Five Crown whiskey. Sometimes George would reveal one of these hiding places to me, saying "Look here," with a sly smile that was his code for a secret.

Sometimes, to make it more exciting, George would partially withdraw a bottle from its hiding place, like a magician making something appear from a hat. He would, at the same time, put a finger to his lips indicating silence. Drinking was not just an emotional pleasure for George, it was also a game, a contest of wits with his mother.

It was no secret to Ada, of course, that her son drank. After forty years of detecting booze on his breath, she had come to regard his drinking as a problem no worse than a case of epilepsy. Some day it might kill him, but in the meantime, it was only producing occasional harmless seizures.

All of this seemed to be the very yeast of life to me, with my own household so righteously proper.

$$\cdots\cdots\cdots\cdots\cdots 6$$

THE music came from the direction of Uptown and threaded through the evening air, not at the level of my ears, but lower, like wisps of sound rising from the ground. I'd heard something like this before, probably in a church I thought, but not here in the Territory, certainly not in the twilight on Maple Street. It was a strange sound, without tempo, not part of the natural orchestra of the countryside, but a faint cry that seemed to fade and then gather strength to cry again.

I ran toward the sound, but when I arrived at the edge of the road, I couldn't hear it any better. It seemed to come from beyond the first hollow. Then in another moment or two, I could hear it more clearly. It grew full of strength and sadness as a little man shouldering bagpipes marched over the rise.

Bagpipes! Ridiculous, I thought. Not *here.*

He was wearing a tweed suit, rumpled but clean, with a complete shirt and tie and strong brown shoes with heavy soles and a cap that fit his head as if a great hand had pressed it down. The wooden pipes of his instrument were as worn as the handles of old axes and the cloth of the bag was mottled with age. His stride was as deliberate as if he were

leading a parade and his face was reddened from pumping
the air.

He passed close by where I stood, but didn't seem to see
me. There was no letup in the infinite, persistent notes that
shrilled from the pipes. He was old, I could see, but appeared
strong and even a little menacing. He had bristling eyebrows
and large knuckles in his fingers. There was no way to tell
if he might be capable of a smile or a snarl, for his mouth
was straight-lipped at its work.

I followed along in stride with him, walking past my house
and then beyond. It was as if there were just the two of us
in the whole Territory then, with no one else even aware of
this stranger passing through, no one but me. The notes
continued to pour from the pipes, each emerging separately,
then falling together like organ chords.

I had certainly never seen this man before, not in my
neighborhood or anywhere else around town. Who could he
be? Why was he playing bagpipes on a country road on a
summer night? Was he some sort of traveling minstrel who
would soon stop and ask me for money?

I felt in my pockets, but there were no coins there.

When we came to a place on the road where there were
no houses, the piper slowed his steps and turned to see who
was tagging along. He let the last notes of the music trail
from the pipes, although he was no longer putting his wind
into the bag.

He seemed to be enjoying the mystery of himself.

"Where do you come from?" I asked.

"You haven't seen me before?" he answered, amused at
the attention I was paying him.

"Never. Have you been here before?"

"Oh, yes," the piper said. "I knew your father . . ."

"What's your name?"

"It doesn't matter," he said. "Names don't matter in my business."

"I don't understand. Do you live around here?"

"Sometimes," he said. "But it isn't where I'm *from* that's important, it's where I'm free to *go.*" He was smiling still.

I was trying to think of another question when the piper hitched up the weight of his pipes. But as he wet his lips and took a deep breath, I knew that would be the end of talking.

"Will you come again?" I asked anyway.

The old man nodded his answer. He was blowing his pipes again and his cheeks were puffing up under his eyes. Then the music began and he went on down the road.

It was almost dark when I turned to walk home. I felt as if I'd just had an encounter with a character out of a book, perhaps even a fairy tale.

7

IF I hadn't been a day hop, I might actually have liked the Academy. I had to admit it really wasn't such a bad place. It had nice old ivy-covered buildings and there was a big dining room with tablecloths and a chapel with an organ and a library and a gym that had ropes and rings hanging down from the ceiling. The thing that was wrong with the Academy as far as I was concerned were the boarding students. They just didn't seem to understand hard times or even know they existed. (This fit right in with my theory that the Depression probably hadn't yet spread to all parts of the United States and might never.) Boarding students had two tennis racquets and portable battery radios in leather cases and their own study lamps, the kind with flexible goose necks. And the girls walked around campus carrying fashion magazines along with their notebooks. I used to think that if some of these kids ever got a chance look at Across-the-street, they'd probably think it was a foreign country.

I took all the usual stuff in class, English, Algebra, Civics and made passable grades and got along with my teachers okay, although I don't think I was anyone's favorite student. If I had a favorite teacher, it was Miss Latham who taught French and was also the school librarian. She was young and blonde and sort of pretty and she passed me in French even if I didn't seem to know beans about grammar. She said my accent was surprisingly good. I never told her about my trip to Europe.

One afternoon in May, I decided it was as good a time as any to start planning specifically for my big summer move. Up to now all I'd done was daydream about running away without really thinking of how it was going to be done, where I was going to, and important things like that. I figured the library might be a good place to start looking for information about places to go, so after my last class I wandered in to see Miss Latham.

The library was small and oak paneled and everything in it was compact and organized. Miss Latham sat at one end of the room behind a small oak desk and when some student wasn't asking for her help she was usually reading a book. She looked up when I asked her about road maps.

"You mean an atlas?" she said, keeping her voice low like you were supposed to.

"Well, yes," I said, "anything that shows highways and places to go."

"What part of the country are you interested in?" she asked, very businesslike, as if there was nothing strange at all about a fourteen-year-old picking out some part of the United States to run away to.

"Well, all I wanted to do was look at any map, really," I said awkwardly.

"There's no such creature as *any* map, Charles," she said teasingly. "It has to be a *someplace* map."

"How about the South Seas," I said, trying to think of something quickly. Bora Bora. Pitcairn. French Frigate Shoals. What names!

"But you said a road map. They don't have roads between

those islands, you know." Now she was teasing me for sure and she seemed even prettier than usual.

"Aw, I don't care, Miss Latham," I said, giving up all pretense. "I just like to look at places I might go, faraway, interesting places."

"Well, let's see now," she said, putting her glasses back on and changing her voice to sound very proper and official. "When did you plan on leaving, young man?"

Why couldn't I just go into the library and find what I wanted myself, I thought? I was feeling more foolish every minute I stood at Miss Latham's desk.

"If you're leaving as soon as school is over, you might consider a summer trip to Tibet," she went on. "That's far away and interesting and they have some very big mountains there. Do you like to climb?"

"I was thinking of places in this country," I said, hoping she would stop making fun of me.

"Well, in this country we have Yellowstone Park and the Grand Canyon and Niagara Falls," she said. She was smiling again now.

"Sorry, Miss Latham," I said finally. "I didn't mean to bother you."

"It's no bother," she said. "You just have to make up your mind. Why don't you go to some of the gasoline stations in town and ask them for maps. They're free."

I could feel the big smile starting to spread across my face almost as soon as she said it. That was it! That was *exactly* it! The Gulf station! Socony! Tydol! They all had maps, road maps, maps with mileages on them and all sorts of information for someone who might be, say, hitchhiking a long way from home. New York City. Indianapolis. Walla Walla.

"Thank *you*, Miss Latham!" I said out loud.

"Shhh," she said, putting a finger to her lips.

"That's a keen idea," I added, more softly.

"Glad to be of service," she said, smiling prettily again. Then she beckoned me closer to her, flexing her index finger as if to pull me right up to her face. The nailpolish on her fingernail matched her lipstick.

"One more question," she said very softly. "Are those maps going to be for a class project or are you up to something?"

For an instant I didn't know whether she was being a friend or a teacher. Miss Latham could be sort of in between. When she caught kids smoking, she didn't always turn them in, I knew that.

"I'm planning a trip," I said, hoping that would be enough of an answer.

"Alone?"

"I don't know yet."

"Could I come too?" She really had a beautiful smile, I thought. Her lipstick was a sort of peach color.

"Any time, Miss Latham!" I said, laughing and pretending to go along with her tease.

"Shhh," she said again. "Do you want everyone to know?"

Then she winked at me.

_8_

•••••••••••••••••••

EACH May there came a day when I was sent to get what would be my last haircut of the school year. I remember this because it was a landmark of sorts, a happy event because of what it signified—summer was coming. I knew there would be still a month of school left, of course, but the May haircut was like the beginning of the end. After it was done, it seemed I wouldn't have to go back to John's barbershop for a whole year. Actually, it would only be until the end of August and then I would have to go again.

The time between these haircuts was summer.

There were two barbershops in Hancock, one in the basement of the bank building where the businessmen went for their haircuts and one, in a poorer part of town, which was the one-man domain of John the Turk. That's where Mother said I must go for my haircuts because John charged 30 cents and even that was a lot of money in 1936. Mother didn't know that John also sold contraceptives at the barbershop, gave advice on the treatment of clap and was the contact man for a local woman who did abortions.

John the Turk wasn't just called a Turk, he was from Turkey, although his family had departed a region he called

Anatolia when John was only a small boy. Somehow, in some long-ago migration, they had all arrived in Hancock, Massachusetts. Now John was a fat old man who didn't bother to wear a barber's smock and who breathed heavily of garlic as he cut hair. I don't think he had more than four customers a day, except on Saturdays. Most of the time he could be seen sitting in his own barber chair reading a newspaper.

His shop was on a corner and had large plate glass windows. It had been an Italian bakery at some earlier time and the glass cases for displaying bread, pies and cakes were still at one end of the barbershop. Magazines and newspapers, some in foreign languages, were parked on top of the bakery cases; and on the shelves, behind the slanting glass fronts, John displayed Wildroot, Lucky Tiger and other hair tonic bottles, most of them empty.

Whenever I arrived for a haircut, John's first question was always, "You want *shumpoo* today, boy?" The answer to this had to be no, because a *shumpoo* cost 25 cents when done with soap and 30 cents if an egg were added. The egg method was one of John's specialties.

"Egg good for you," he would say, giving me a slap on the shoulder. "Make hair grow! Make scalp healthy!"

I sometimes wondered just how John would have managed to give a *shumpoo* if I had said I wanted one. The shop had only the barest of professional equipment: a mirror on the wall, a small sink, a barber chair that had come from a dentist's office, and a stubby broom for sweeping hair cuttings into a pile in the corner.

"No *shumpoo* today? Too bad!" John would say, taking the electric clippers from a hook on the wall and blowing garlic on them as he flipped the switch. "Hair needs egg for strength."

John had many theories about strength, health and the

general well-being of growing boys. I imagined that many of these must have come from Turkey because there was nothing like them anywhere else around Hancock. For example, John's assertion that a boy never really filled out all his muscles properly until after his first intercourse with a woman.

"You getta good piece ass, you fill out after that, boy!" he'd say and I would nod solemnly, watching myself in the mirror and trying to maintain a worldly look on my face. Then John would pinch the muscles of my shoulder through the covering of the striped barber's apron and explain that *fooking* was more important than vitamins or anything else, even garlic, in the development of strength and the purification of young blood. Through the whine of the clippers' motor, John rumbled on with advice.

"You think John don't know, but he know. You need piece ass, boy! Right?" And then he would roar with laughter. I could feel an embarrassed smile making my lips turn slightly at the corners.

"You want me to fix you up, boy?"

"Nah, John, thanks. I'm okay." Then, to change the subject I'd tell him to just wet my hair with water; and I'd give the old man his thirty cents and say goodbye. Tipping John the Turk was unheard of, for me at least. All the same, I always wished I had an extra dime to give him.

I knew that John's great ambition, if he could ever get a few dollars ahead, was to buy a second barberchair. Then, he said, he would have a Two Chair Shop, which, in his trade, was apparently a measure of importance and success, like the number of cylinders in a car's engine.

What John thought he would do with two chairs when he didn't have enough business for one was something I didn't understand; nevertheless he had the second chair all picked

42

out. It could be seen anytime in the back room of Bechtel's Swap Shop where Herman Bechtel sometimes sat in it while eating his lunch. It had come from a barbershop that had gone out of business after a bad flood in nearby Woonsocket, Rhode Island.

"But Herman wants $50 for it," John said. "He'd probably sell it for ten, but he knows I want it, so the price stays at fifty. I don't think I'll ever make it."

On my way home from the May haircut I started thinking about getting "fixed up," as John called it. I was still a virgin, although I would never have called myself such a thing. Virginity was another of those categories, one reserved primarily for girls I thought. Like most other categories, I didn't necessarily want to belong to it. I knew there were boys only a little older than I who claimed they already had what John called their first piece and maybe they had. The thought of such a thing filled me with wonder.

Sometimes I thought that if I ran away from Hancock, I might somehow also run away from the virginity category, but I wasn't sure.

.... *9*

ONE of the places I liked to go was the railroad station. There was something about the station that set it apart from the town, a sort of off-limits feeling. I liked to think that if a policeman or my mother or a school teacher should come and catch me smoking there, they would have no jurisdiction because it was railroad property. That's what all the signs said, No Trespassing, Railroad Property. Danger, High Voltage. It didn't belong to Hancock. A different authority prevailed—the New Haven Railroad.

Alf Perry was the ticket agent. He was a Hancock man, but because he worked for the railroad he seemed more worldly than most town people. Alf used to tell me about such famous trains as the Twentieth Century Limited and the Commodore Vanderbilt and he knew where they all went and on what schedule. He even gave me a bunch of New York Central and Pennsylvania Railroad timetables. I studied these and saw that a train could take you just about anywhere in 1936. I liked to think about that.

I had started smoking in the spring. Some of the other fourteen-year-olds at the Academy had been smoking longer. I knew they were ahead of me, that it was going to take a while before I learned to like it. The smoke brought tears to

44

my eyes, but I tried earnestly anyway, as if it was necessary to suffer a little in order to grow up—also necessary to puff hard to keep the cigarettes burning. They were Chesterfields, what Mother smoked. She never missed a couple at a time.

Only a few trains a day stopped in Hancock. Two went to Boston in the morning and two rattled back at night. Others went through to places in Connecticut and one or two of these connected with trains that went 'way out west.

Between trains, Alf Perry usually locked up the station and there was never anybody around in the middle of the afternoon. I used to sit on one of the big, high-wheeled baggage carts parked on the platform. From this perch, I could look down the right of way in both directions. The shining rails materialized from the distance like a mirage, passed through Hancock as if they didn't care whether a town was there or not, then vanished again in the direction of Boston, only 30 miles away.

There were also some express trains that thundered through town on those tracks without even slowing for a signal. Sometimes I waited for an express and put pennies on the rails and watched as the coins were transformed into fragile copper wafers by the locomotive's pounding wheels. I tried the same thing with an old Ingersoll watch once too. That was interesting. I stopped time itself that day. At exactly ten minutes before two. The hands of the watch were still perfectly visible and undistorted after the train went over it but the face was swollen like a full moon.

Another time I let an express crush the holy medal Mother said she had bought at the Vatican in Rome on her travels. The holy medal was only aluminum so it didn't seem to me very holy. After the train passed over it, the image of St. Christopher was completely gone. I wondered if he went to heaven or to Boston on the wheels of the train.

The expresses shook the whole station as they passed, flexing the rails with their weight and power, pumping the track spikes up and down in the old ties like loose teeth, pushing a cloud of rusty dust and dried toilet paper against the weeds on the embankment and leaving behind the smell of oil and hot brake shoes. To me, this was the perfume of adventure.

Sometimes I wondered when the expresses crashed by if there would be any way to stop one. Probably not even Alf Perry could do that. They always went through as if they had important business elsewhere. Sometimes I imagined they were troop trains carrying elements of the Wehrmacht to new positions along the frontiers.

If you lived in Hancock, it was always someplace else that was more important.

The way I was beginning to figure things, there could only be two ways to leave town: by hitchhiking or by train. Neither was perfect. The trouble with hitchhiking was that it might be too easy to get caught, to get picked up and brought home right away, maybe even the first day, and I certainly didn't want that. If I ran away and stayed away for months, maybe years, and then was found, I wouldn't care; I'd be grown up and gone. But if they caught me right away and brought me back, it would certainly be humiliating and I wouldn't want to hear Mother carry on.

I had picked up more than a dozen gasoline company road maps by now and had them all stashed away with my railroad timetables. I had New York, New Jersey, the New England States, United States East of the Mississippi and others. Some maps made it all look easy, like you could just follow a certain red line for a while and then you'd be in Miami or Columbus, Ohio, just as quick as that. The only trouble was, I'd never hitchhiked anywhere in my life and I wasn't sure how to do it. One thing I knew: hitchhiking meant that you had to spend a lot of time along the side of the road with your thumb up and if you were a missing person and the cops were all looking for you, it seemed like a pretty easy way to get caught.

On the other hand, I didn't see how they could ever catch me if I took the train. Of course, most of the trains that stopped in Hancock just went to Boston and everybody who got aboard was only going to Boston and would know everybody else. I tried to picture how it would be if I just got on one of those trains some morning. Some friend of Mother's would surely recognize me and ask what it was that took me to Boston all by myself. And then I'd say . . . what *would* I say? I couldn't very well explain that I was running away from home, that I was never coming back to this crummy place.

I thought about hopping a freight, too, but somehow that seemed risky although you were always reading about kids who hopped freights and went from one hobo jungle to the next without any trouble at all. Unfortunately, the only freight trains I'd ever seen around Hancock were just delivering coal to sidings and they crawled in and out of town about ten miles and hour and probably ended up in West Virginia.

The best thing would be a train that went from Hancock to, say, Chicago. A big train, an important train, with nobody on it from around here. No such train stopped in Hancock, of course, but I still dreamed about the possibility. Suppose a train just made an *unscheduled* stop, one that was lost or switched to the wrong track and had to come through Hancock because there was no other way, like a detour. I thought that probably happened more often than passengers realized. If they got aboard in, say, New York and were going to Michigan, would they necessarily know their train shouldn't be passing through a town called Hancock? I thought people like that, important people, would hardly notice because they'd be so busy talking and reading and eating and drinking in the dining car. So maybe it was possible after all that someday, somehow, there would be some unscheduled train I could take, some long string of fancy coaches that would stop here at last.

It would come toward the station like all those other expresses that didn't stop, its headlamp gleaming down the tracks fiercely, almost hypnotically, even in daylight. Seen head on, the engine would pitch and sway as it approached. But then, instead of running right through town with all its wheels crying like iron violins, this train would slow and then stop at the empty depot.

First down from the cars would be the Pullman porters, in their white jackets and shiny brown skulls, some descending all the way to the roadbed, others leaning from open doorways, looking up the tracks, talking and gesturing. Then the length of the waiting train would be paced off by a conductor and trainman who would walk along the roadbed by the coaches like ringmasters, all in elegant uniforms with gold braid and gold watch chains across vests with gold buttons. I could hear them talking about signal blocks and other reasons for the delay while they studied their watches with lordly impatience. Up ahead, the great locomotive would stand chuffing smoke and hissing steam from a dozen places, an impatient giant detained in the wilderness. At the other end of the train was an observation car with gleaming brass railing and special lights and lanterns and flags, lacking only a movie star or a presidential candidate. Big Negroes wearing tall white chef's hats leaned from a dining car's open kitchen door and laughed and spit down at the tracks while passengers having a late lunch sat at linen-covered tables with real flowers and conversed as they ate, never looking out the windows at whatever place this was where a signal had stopped the train and a boy sat on a baggage cart, watching.

That's when I could hop down and stride easily toward the steps of one of the Pullman cars. The best place to go first would be the dining car, I planned, so I turned that way, opening door after door between the cars until I came to one all trimmed in brass with a fancy frosted glass window that said Dining Car and was all polished walnut paneling and white linen inside. There was a polite man in a uniform who asked if I was alone. I said yes and he showed me to a table by one of the windows where white china and shining glassware was already set and three carnations stood brightly in a thin vase. Then a Negro waiter came and gave me a big smile and said, "Yas, sir!" as he slipped open a menu for me.

All the while, of course, I didn't want to look out the window because I knew I wasn't really free yet. Hancock was still right there, the same station platform where I'd watched so many other trains pass, but now I was on one of them and pretty soon it would start to roll, quietly, powerfully, secretly.

I told the Negro waiter that I wanted a package of Chesterfields while I decided what to choose from the menu and he said Yas, sir! again and went to get the cigarettes.

Then the train started to move forward.

.... *10*

EVEN though I reassured myself over and over that running away was a kid's basic right, I had to admit that it was a matter serious enough only to be done under certain justifiable circumstances. That was a problem. I didn't want my disappearance to look like just a childish stunt. After I was gone, I wanted everybody to understand that what I did made sense. *He had a right,* that's what I wanted people to say. For that reason, I spent a lot of time putting together mental lists of what I thought were good reasons for running away from Hancock: (1) the place was too small; (2) it was poverty stricken; (3) it was ugly; (4) it didn't even have a movie theatre any more; and (5) nothing ever happened in Hancock, nothing important that is, only small time stuff, the sort of things I used to hear Mother gossiping about.

After I run away, I said to myself, if anyone asks me why I left such a nice old New England town where my distinguished old family lived for centuries, I'll be able to tell them what I know about nice old New England towns. Boy, will I! About old Mr. Winter who used to be a conductor on the railroad and got fired because he got caught stealing tickets. Or that Chinese woman who ran the Bluebird Lounge out on the highway and probably sold opium, at least that's what they said. Or the man who ran a shoe store who was horse-whipped right on the main street by some woman's husband. (Horsewhipping was supposed to be legal in Massachusetts under certain circumstances, I gathered, although I didn't understand why.) Then there was the pretty Armenian girl who drank disinfectant and died before the fire department could get her to the hospital. One of Mother's friends said the girl was pregnant, but she wasn't married, so maybe that was the problem, although it seemed there were always rumors about girls being pregnant in Hancock.

There was moonshine made in Hancock too, and the furniture store fire was suspected of being arson and the town's only eye doctor had once been accused of molesting a woman while the lights were turned down in his examining room. I heard a lot about *that* case because the woman was one of our neighbors.

I thought all of these adult scandals could be lumped together and added to my list as #6—"Hancock is full of weird old people who do weird things."

Sometimes I wondered if my mother might belong on that list too. I guessed she really was what she said she was, an Investment Counselor, but I still didn't understand what she meant when she said she didn't actually sell stocks to people. "I only sell them dreams," she'd say with a sad smile.

Across-the-street Ada used to simply say, "Your ma's in stocks." Other people usually referred to Mother's business as "stocks and bonds." But Mother insisted on calling herself an Investment Counselor, which certainly sounded more like a category than a job. The phrase must have had a ring to it that she preferred to "stock broker." Mother liked words that had an important sound about them. When she talked to her customers on the telephone, she was always using such terms as "liquid capital" and "money velocity" and "technical correction." I was sure the customers must be impressed, but I wondered if they understood.

If I was in the house when Mother was talking business with her customers on the phone, I was supposed to keep very quiet or get out of the way. Nevertheless, I often overheard and some of what my ears caught was puzzling. For example, sometimes I'd hear Mother tell someone that she was calling from her "office," or that she was away from her "desk," or that something was "in the files." These remarks always struck me as odd because she did all her business from a big overstuffed chair in the living room and there was no office or desk or files, just a small table with the telephone on it and many copies of the *Boston Herald* folded open to the stock quotation pages.

All the same, there was no question about it, Mother had lots of customers and she spent a good many hours every day talking to people about stocks. And she was a bona fide broker. She had a connection with a proper firm in Boston, although she always complained that the "home office" didn't let her use any stationery with the company name on it.

One of Mother's frequent declarations of fact went, "Some of the most important people in this town are your mother's customers. They have respect for what I know. They certainly wouldn't trust me with their money if they thought I was a crook!" I would always agree with this by solemnly nodding my head. Failure to make some affirmative response could very well bring on the What-do-you-mean-by-not-answering-me? rebuke.

Needless to say, the stock-and-bond business must have been very bad everywhere in 1936, but it surely had to be worse in Hancock with all the mills closed down and everybody out of work. All the same, Mother kept trying. I remember that many of her customers were what she called, somewhat disdainfully, "odd lotters," meaning they could only afford to buy five or ten shares at a time. They were people who were hoping to make a few extra dollars on gambles they couldn't afford, but didn't dare pass up either, especially after Mother told them what an opportunity they might be missing.

Mother said she wasn't going to let the Depression lick *her,* so she made her pitch to anyone, anytime. "You never know who's got some money put away," she'd say with the true optimism of a gold prospector. She even tried to sell people like Mr. LeBlanc, the man with the team of horses.

One of Mother's best customers, even in the Depression, was a man called Big Tony Ferrara. He was in the grocery business and used to make bets that he could walk up the Town Hall steps carrying a hundred-pound sack of potatoes in each hand. Tony weighed almost 300 pounds himself and when he came to our house to talk stocks, which he did sometimes in the evening, he would often bring Mother a small wooden box of Italian macaroons.

One day, Mother discovered a Canadian gold mine stock that she told all her customers would be a "marvelous opportunity for capital appreciation," meaning, I supposed, that they would make a lot of money on it. (I remember that an announcement of this sort always sent a thrill through the house. Mother had what we called a New Good One!) I think this new good one was called Red Feather Mines, something like that, and although Mother acknowledged that it wasn't exactly producing gold just yet, the engineers had made many tests and the "indication" was that they were sitting on top of a very big vein of gold, very big indeed.

What I couldn't figure out was how Mother learned about things like the Red Feather Mine (or any of her other New

Good Ones) when she hardly ever went out of the house except to go Uptown each day to get her mail and the *Boston Herald*. I might have asked her how news of a Canadian gold mine had found its way to Hancock, Massachusetts, but I knew that would only bring on the People-in-this-town-trust-me declaration again and might even end with the grim second warning that, "When I'm gone, I hope you'll realize how much I was respected!"

When *I'm* gone, I thought, I hope Hancock will understand why I left—and to prepare for that day I now began collecting emergency rations for my journey. I had a box of seedless raisins and a box of graham crackers put away already. I thought I should probably get some marshmallows and Milky Ways too. As for that staple of all hobo jungles, Mulligan stew, I didn't know whether I could find it in cans.

54

11

I KNEW for several days that something must be dead somewhere near our house. There was a signal in the spring air that came and went like a faint warning, a wisp now and then, thin as a cobweb. One end reached my nostrils and the other end trailed off . . . to where? I couldn't tell. It drifted.

I had a good nose for what was in the wind; for me smells were a source of information, just as they were for animals. I knew the scent rain makes before it falls. At night, I could always catch the smell of a kerosene lantern, even far off. I could walk past a stack of drying cordwood and know what was in it—oak or black birch or mulberry. Snow had a certain smell too, and rusting iron and wet shingles and hens. And of course, anything dead, like an old woodchuck wedged in a wall.

The new smell was like that, *dead,* and it varied from a faint perfume, like blossoms, to something strong and ripe, like cheese. I calculated that it came from somewhere north of our house, northeast a little, maybe. After a few days of being just curious, I decided to follow my nose.

If our big old house with all its windows and doors and fireplaces and brick ovens and handmade door latches was Mother's domain, then the woods and fields around the

55

house were mine. I knew that the land beyond our own acres actually belonged to others, but boundary lines didn't really matter. There were hundreds of wilderness acres in *my* Territory and even if it were someone else's property legally, it was mine to use.

This Territory was not part of the town, nor was it Maple Street either. It was a private wilderness, a place where I felt sovereign. It had its own loose boundaries and within these there were, I imagined, Indian footpaths and pioneer wagon trails, playing fields and amphitheatres, earthworks and battlefields, dens and caves, watchtowers and burial grounds. I knew them all like places on a familiar map or like the rooms in my house.

I had explored this secret Territory in all seasons. I knew where to find high-bush blueberries in summer, or the herb called Golden Heart in fall; I harvested pussywillow in spring and fresh, green watercress even in December. I knew where old broken wagon wheels or discarded shovels lay half buried or where loops of rusted barbed wire were left from old battles. I could find a certain tree with heavy iron bolts mysteriously ingrown in its trunk (was this where they had kept the prisoners?) and a strange, man-made depression, all lined with stones, which I called the Indian Grave. I knew where the shapeliest young pines could be found for Christmas trees. I knew where owls lived and woodchucks and black snakes and bats. And, of course, where my friends the red ants were preparing for war.

The Main Street of my woodland Territory was Mr. Le-Blanc's Wagon Path that cut through the woods for about a half a mile between Maple Street and Oak Street. You couldn't call it a road, just two parallel wheel tracks pressed into the forest floor, packed hard and worn smooth by the frequent passage of a heavy farm wagon. It was a gently turning, up and down trail that followed the contours of the land and went easily around obstacles. It was really Mr. LeBlanc's two horses that had determined the route in the beginning. He was the only person who used the path and had pioneered it as a shortcut through the woods for himself, even though none of the land it passed through was his. No trees had been downed to make the path and no earth had been scraped or filled. Only the grass in the wheel ruts had given up its right of way to the comings and goings of the old French-Canadian farmer and his big team. If the owners knew of this trespass, they didn't seem to mind. It was just "LeBlanc's Path."

LeBlanc's Path had its own landmarks: the place where the partridges often hid in the leaves, the spot where the old broken medicine bottles made a sparkly pile of blue glass at the base of a lichen-green stone wall, the slope where Mother and I came in December to pick the evergreen ground covers that we used to make Christmas wreaths. I knew them all.

Wherever I went alone in my Territory, I always felt confident and independent. I might squirm trying to make conversation with one of the girls at the Academy, and in the house I was still treated like a child, but in these woods I felt grown up. Much older than fourteen. I knew how to walk silently, how to listen, how to see. I could find my way through thick stands of young pine or rough brush as surely and effortlessly as any of the creatures that lived there. I believed the woods were a sanctuary and that, if need be, I could run to them for safety.

There wasn't anything but some old rundown farms between our house and the north end of Maple Street. So when I set out to try and track down the strange odor, it was late in the afternoon. The sun was on its way down behind a ridge of trees to the west. I walked past the old Corbin place, which wasn't even a farm, and then past the house where Mrs. Claflin, the lady who had been molested by the eye doctor, lived. After that it was all pretty much scrub land until I came to Navotny's sawmill. Navotny was the crazy one who told everyone who would listen that F.D.R. was a Jew. I had a dream once about Navotny coming to saw me end to end.

I kept walking, but not too fast. I believed that if you ran after a scent, you could lose it.

I wondered whether anyone else on the street had noticed this smell. There were plenty of other rancid odors around. Navotny kept goats, for example and they could make a great stink, and then, if the wind was right, you could often smell the garbage slop from the pig farm that the Armenian ran down at the end of the road. The Armenian was blind. I wasn't sure of his name. People just called him The Armenian.

No cars passed me on the road, there was no one in sight. Some crows perched in tall pines behind old man Winter's house. The tops of the trees swayed slightly in puffy winds, but down on the ground everything was still. The smell was more definite now.

The house had no driveway because Winter never owned a car. After all those years of being a railroad conductor and riding only on trains, I supposed he hadn't learned about cars. He hadn't married either. He lived alone and used to walk a mile and a half to town a couple of times a week, pulling a kid's express wagon for his groceries. It had the name "Peerless" lettered on the side in red. His old clapboard farmhouse sat far back from the road and high on a ridge. It must have had a nice front lawn once, before the Town had widened and blacktopped Maple Street. That was when Winter let the Town dig out the gravel they needed from his front yard—not as a gift, but for a good price, George said. (In the 1930s, people would sell anything for money, even their front lawns.) As a result, Winter's house always looked as if it were standing high on the edge of a sandy cliff, a sea captain's house atop a dune, facing a sea that was never there.

Mr. Winter always wore a sad, gray look, a black suit with a white shirt and a vest. Just as if he were still a conductor on the New Haven. I was scared of him.

What was most interesting about Winter, however, was the story about his being a crook and getting fired from the railroad for taking passengers' tickets and selling them over again, unpunched. He'd done it for years before he got caught, they said. I wondered if he had made much money from this scheme. Mr. Winter always looked like the poorest man in town.

I cut from the road, bearing up the grade to the right, following the lip of the gravel pit, aiming my steps for the back of the house. I knew if the old man saw me coming across his land, he'd holler, but my curiosity and the smell had hold of me. Even fear of old man Winter couldn't stop me now.

A clothesline reached from the corner post of the back porch to the corner of the barn behind the house. A single dishtowel flapped on the line, the only sign that someone might live there. The place always looked that way. I stepped up onto the porch. The screen door was ajar, but the inner door was closed. A single window on the porch looked into what I thought was probably the kitchen. I cupped my hands to the glass and tried to see into the gloom of the house. There was no sound, but what had been only an elusive and mysterious scent a quarter mile up the road was now such a smell that it had *thickness.* It pumped at my stomach.

What was left of Mr. Winter was melted into an old over-stuffed chair, the head slumped forward, a tuft of gray hair sticking out at the top of the pile. I'd never seen a dead person before and I didn't know how long it took for one to get this far gone, but it was like looking at something that you weren't supposed to see, a development that took place much later, after the funeral, below ground, when everyone was gone.

The burrowing of maggots made Winter stir slightly in his chair, as if he were still trying, feebly, to get up.

Naturally, discovering a dead man caused a great commotion, not just when the police came and then Dr. Hersey with the fire department, but for days afterwards people were talking about old man Winter and how long he might have been there and who last saw him alive. Police Sergeant Barrett asked me some questions about how it was that I happened to be on Winter's back porch and I said I was just poking around after school, doing nothing in particular. I didn't say anything about following the smell. This excuse didn't please Mother much because she said a well-brought-up boy wouldn't be trespassing on other people's property like that and she thought it reflected poorly on her in some way, but I could see I wasn't going to get into any bad trouble about it. Everybody knew that if I'd been up to mischief at the Winter place, I would have just slipped away and said nothing about seeing the old man's body.

The next day George said, "You sure got quite a nose for trouble, ain't you, boy?" It sounded like he was scolding me.

"Well," I said, "you're the one who always told me to pay attention to smells!" Actually, I was proud of my keen senses and the discovery they had led me to.

George had dry leaves in his throat. They rustled when he

tried to laugh and turned into a cough. "Regular little tracker, aren't you?" he went on, his old grape eyes sliding onto mine. "When are you goin' to follow the trail of that Wendell girl into the woods?" I knew George's look was intended to have a double meaning. "I see you talkin' to her," he said.

For a moment I didn't know whether George was suggesting an idea I'd already thought of myself or not. Maybe something like it *had* already occurred to me. Maybe I had thought about walking with the Wendell girl along LeBlanc's path, say. But even if I had, I didn't want to talk about it with George. He just snickered at everything.

My mother's final theory on the Winter case was that if the old man had traveled, he wouldn't have shut himself in like that. "Ignorance is all it is," she said after a few days. "They'll never find *me* like that," she went on, holding a small mackerel up by the tail before lowering its flour-coated body into a frying pan.

"When was it exactly that we went to Europe?" I asked. It always seemed as if Mother's travels must have happened centuries ago.

"We came home on the *Laconia* in 1928," she said, turning her head to one side so the spatter from the frying wouldn't get on her glasses. Mother still wore the Woodrow Wilson kind that clipped onto her nose. "Oh, that was such a lovely trip . . ."

"That's eight years ago," I said. "We've been here for eight years?"

"Well, you have to remember, there's a Depression." The smell of the fish was beginning to fill the kitchen with an oily nausea.

It always came down to the Depression. It was all anybody talked about. It was the reason for everything, the cause of everything, the excuse for everything. Mother's 1928 Hudson, for example. She said she couldn't trade it for a new car as long as there was a Depression. It was true, Mother had put only 16,000 miles on the car in eight years. About the same mileage as Mr. Winter's express wagon, I thought dejectedly, and all of it just between Maple Street and Uptown. So far as I knew, the car had never been to Boston. I didn't think Mother knew the way.

It was quarter to seven. On the radio, Lowell Thomas told how Haile Selassie had arrived at the League of Nations and Alf Landon was going to run against F.D.R., but Lowell Thomas never mentioned the mysterious death of Mr. Winter in Hancock, Massachusetts.

I ate most of the mackerel, but not the soft brown part.

••••••••••••••••••• *12*

ONE thing I had no love for was mowing the lawn. The grass always came up so fast and thick in May that I could scarcely keep ahead of it. By July, thanks to heat and drought, there was hardly any lawn left, but the weeds then flourished instead, led by one variety that went to seed on tall stalks (my mother called these "pollywogs" for some reason) which the push-mower could not cut. By fall the grass came back again, green and cold, and grew up through the dry, brown leaves. Raking was then added to mowing as one of my required chores.

Being fourteen and in charge of what Mother called The Estate was even worse punishment than it was when I was thirteen. I would be big enough this summer, she said, to do all sorts of jobs—but too young, she added, to go anywhere on my own, not even to camp in Maine any more. Every good reason was given for this situation, mostly the Depression. (It depressed everything.) Also family tradition, which apparently required us to keep on doing things just the way they had always been done before my father died. Third was what I called the Categories. So many things came in categories, it seemed, and they had a lot to do with the way life was organized and how things turned out. Even lawns came in categories.

For example, there were such things as power lawn mowers in 1936—there was a beauty at the hardware store Uptown for only $150—but we didn't own one. Ours was a balky, hand-pushed contraption with iron wheels and a wooden roller in back. The only places lucky enough to have power mowers were the Union Street Cemetery, the Academy, the Golf Club and some of the big houses Uptown, the ones with lawns that stayed smooth and green and were sprinkled all summer. These were in the Power Mower category and, oh, the music of those gasoline engines and the shearing song of the blades cutting grass (and pollywogs!) while the driver did nothing but ride along behind.

We just weren't in this category, nor anywhere near it. Our country lawn had expanded outward from the house mostly as a result of mowing and raking a little deeper into the surrounding fields each spring. Mother insisted on a certain amount of progress in this work every year. It was as if she were pushing back the wilderness and replacing it, yard by yard, with civilization—that is, mowed grass. Consequently, most of our lawn was made up of various kinds of weeds and wildflowers or mossy patches, but when it was all fresh cut at the same time, it looked much the same as a proper lawn. Especially in the evening when the sun was low and the light made everything look golden soft. I liked our lawn all right, even when I was fourteen. I just didn't like having to work on it.

Bad news came in the spring of 1936. My lawn problem appeared suddenly about to grow worse—even before the young grass started up, I faced a new worry. I heard my mother telling one of her telephone friends that she would soon have a "French gardener" come to do landscaping. She hadn't said anything about this to me, so I didn't know what might be in store, but it sounded odd and made me uneasy.

I didn't see why anyone would have landscaping done in the middle of a Depression anyway. I couldn't imagine what she was up to.

When the "French gardener" came, I was relieved to see that he wasn't French after all, at least not really; it was just Mr. LeBlanc. He had the big farm on Oak Street and the team of horses and he sold milk. He also built stone walls for people and graded land and cut wood and did almost anything else you needed. He'd done jobs for Mother before. He was from Canada originally, I knew, and maybe that made him French, but I didn't think he was really a landscape gardener.

Nevertheless, Mr. LeBlanc was soon pacing off great distances around our house under Mother's directions. He put stakes in the ground all over. Mother was nodding and saying, yes, that's just what she wanted, hedges here and flower beds there and lots of open space. "Open space," I feared, meant more lawn. Mother had been to Versailles once in her travels and I think she had always dreamed of the day when she would transform our Hancock acreage into something equally imposing. Now, apparently, the time had come and Mr. LeBlanc was going to be the man to do it.

"You'll have a good helper here," she said to Mr. LeBlanc, smiling at me in the way she never smiled except in front of other people. "He's strong and he's just like his father, he loves horses."

Mr. LeBlanc was a big man in his fifties, the strongest man I would ever know, I was sure. He had always been a hero to me, a man who could do anything, either with his own strength or with the power of his team.

I'd known Mr. LeBlanc and his horses since I was a little boy. In those days, when I'd hear his team coming down the road, harness jingling and the big iron-clad wheels rumbling and crunching sand on the macadam, I'd run to meet him so I could have a ride.

When he saw me, he would always stop—*whoa Jimmy, whoa Harry*—and as the wagon came to rest with the horses tossing their heads impatiently, I'd get a foot up on the step and Mr. LeBlanc's big hand would grab me under one arm, lift, and next thing I'd be sitting beside him and looking out over the broad hindquarters of the two grays.

It wouldn't be a long ride, only past my own house, just to where he turned off the paved road and into the woods on his wagon path. But to me this was a trip to a far and wonderful land where men like Mr. LeBlanc ruled over such weapons as double-bitted axes and cant-hooks and could push a one-ton horse straight back into its traces if it got balky.

"If you're going to be my helper boy, you'd better eat good," Mr. LeBlanc said, bringing my thoughts back to the present. "What did I tell you to eat to be strong? You remember?"

I remembered. "You said pea soup."

He laughed a big, deep laugh and pushed my head to one side playfully like he sometimes pushed the horses' muzzles. "Not just pea soup, boy! What else?"

"Johnny cake!"

"Right you are! Pea soup and johnny cake!" He had an accent. Maybe it was French after all, I wasn't sure.

All the same, what would have been an event of almost unbearable joy a few years earlier, didn't seem to have the same effect on me in 1936. The fact that Mr. LeBlanc was coming to work at our place should have been as exciting as if a circus was going to perform in the back yard. But it was not. Somehow, I knew this wasn't going to make anything better, wasn't going to change any of the important issues, not My Case Against This Town or My Case Against Private School. Whenever I thought about these grievances, I realized that there probably wasn't another kid I knew who had as many good reasons for running away as I did.

I used to look for places to brood about my fate, places to make plans without being interrupted by the sleigh bell. In addition to the railroad station and the cedar grove, I liked to go into the woods in back of George's house until I came to the small dark pond gouged out of the earth by the crash of the Army plane. The hole was always full of water now and the trees around it were still splintered and smashed as if a tornado had ripped through. There was something mysterious about the hole too. People said the pilot of the plane had never been found, that his body was still there somewhere at the bottom, along with all the wreckage they couldn't pull out. I thought this the saddest thing about the airplane crash. The pilot, whoever he was, would never go back to his airbase again, would never fly any more. This was the last place on earth that he had seen; the pilot would have to stay in Hancock forever.

Airplane Pond was George's fishing hole now, also one of his private drinking spots, too deep in the pine forest for Ada to be able to follow him—and too far for me to hear the sleigh bell.

In an experiment I was sure wasn't going to work, George had stocked the muddy water with some young catfish a few summers ago. Soon, he said, they'd be big enough to eat. I had had some of George's catfish before and they seemed even less palatable than my mother's mackerel. All the same, I went fishing with George any time he asked me, partly because I thought his feelings would be hurt if I refused and partly because the pond was a good place to sit and think.

The pond was actually a cheerless sort of spot, a round

pool surrounded by a brushy shoreline and darkly shaded by woods. Its iron-gray surface was usually unruffled by any breeze. It was easy just to sit and stare at the reflections. George said the water was very deep in the middle.

At the edge of the pond ice skaters had chopped trees and built deadwood fires in winter and it was from this charcoal- and beer-bottle-littered clearing that George always fished. He sat with his back up against a big log and used an old two-piece metal rod, painted black, with a cork handle. For bait he brought earthworms in a milk bottle. He also brought whiskey. Taking swallows from the pint of Seagram's Five Crown was part of the fishing ritual.

One afternoon, George came back from the pond by himself carrying a milk pail that he put down on the barn steps.

"Want to see something?" he said, pointing to the pail.

I stared at two medium-sized catfish circling in discolored pond water.

"Beauties, ain't they?" George said. Their skins were greenish black and their heads broad and their long whiskers swept the bottom of the container that held them captive.

"Going to eat them for supper?" I asked.

George snickered. "Goin' to eat them," he said, "but first I'm goin' to fatten 'em up a bit!"

I didn't know what George meant, but I watched as he carried the pail to the north side of the house where two big oak barrels caught rain water from the roof gutters. Both barrels were nearly full. George hoisted the milk pail to the edge of one barrel and tilted it until the two dark, twisting bodies slithered into the inkwell depths.

"Now we'll give 'em a little pork rind and other scraps and by and by they'll be nice," George said. He seemed pleased with his catch and what he would make of it. I didn't know what "by and by" meant, but I suddenly felt sorry for the

68

fish, imprisoned in the dark barrel. True, the pond they had been taken from was no crystal lake, but it was certainly better than living in a barrel.

"You going to feed them now?" I asked.

"Oh, they'll be all right for a time," George said, taking the milk pail back to the barn.

Later that afternoon I caught a couple of grasshoppers and dropped them into the rain barrel. They floated on the still surface, but no fish came up to get them.

AFTER all the fuss about old man Winter's death had quieted down, his house still fascinated me. As the one who found him, I guess I wanted to go on playing detective. I thought it would be great to find out all I could about the mysterious old hermit who had lived and died alone. There was that rumor about him stealing from the railroad, for example.

A week or so after they had taken the body away I went back to the house for the first time and found the cellar door open. I knew I didn't have any business going inside and Mother had said I should stay away, that I'd already caused enough to-do with my snooping around. But the temptation was strong, even though the police had tacked a legal notice on the front door and put a new hasp and padlock on the back. I understood this meant no one should trespass until Winter's relatives could be located, if he had any. Some people thought he might have some kinfolk living out west, but no one was sure. For the moment, the house belonged to nobody and I decided to go in.

The old cellar door was barely hanging from its rusted hinges; anyone could have pulled it open without having it called breaking and entering. I went down the few steps like a diver entering the hull of a sunken ship. Almost at once, I was surrounded by a damp chill and near darkness. When my eyes became accustomed to the light, I could see that the cellar had an earthen floor and fieldstone walls and was full of junk piled high in boxes everywhere. Cartons of dishes and tools and utensils; clay pots and bottles and coils of wire; stacks of rusty iron pipe and sagging fruit baskets and broken shutters; piles of dusty firewood and bundles of newspapers and bales of cardboard all tied up with string. It was a hermit's collection all right, but pretty much like other accumulations I'd seen in people's cellars. In Hancock, no one ever threw away such things as old stoves or broken toilet bowls or burst inner tubes or burned out motors or bent rat traps or cracked milk pitchers or even one rubber boot. So long as there was a barn or a shed or an attic or a cellar, such things were automatically kept against the day when they might somehow be useful again. "Waste not, want not," was everybody's favorite saying—even Mother's.

A dark staircase led up from the cellar into the house and I groped my way, hands extended to each side, until I came to the door at the top. The knob turned and the door opened into the kitchen—the room where Winter had set himself down for his final rest. Except for a sort of mustiness, the horrid smell wasn't there. The chair in which the old man had died was gone. The green window shades were pulled down.

Just being alone in the old house and seeing everything left in its place was scary. It didn't take much looking around to see that the old man must have hoarded junk for years. Every room was full of it. Stacks of dry kindling reached from the floor almost to the ceiling in the kitchen and yellowing bundles of newspapers were all over. It looked like Winter had lived mostly in two rooms, the kitchen and a combination bedroom-sitting room next to it. The doors to other parts of the house were shut tight.

I only stayed in the house about ten minutes that first time, but it was long enough to look into the kitchen drawers and cabinets and see all the cans of soup and evaporated milk still on the shelves and to find the icebox in the pantry empty. There were a couple of mysteries too. Under the bed I saw a bundle of old umbrellas and on the top shelf of a closet was a shoebox full of eyeglasses, a couple of dozen pairs it looked like, all different and none of them broken. I was sure the place must be full of other fascinating curiosities, but I was beginning to fear I'd been gone from home long enough for Mother to wonder.

I made up my mind to come back to the Winter house as often as I could. It was like being an archaeologist searching for clues to a human existence that had been here and then disappeared. It was also like having a sort of club house all my own.

Along with LeBlanc's path and the Cedar Grove and Airplane Pond, the house became one of my private places. After a while, I discovered that it was an especially great place to be when a summer storm came along, much better than being at home with my mother who was always so scared that she sometimes made me scared too. I was never scared in the Winter house though and sometimes I sat on the back porch just to watch a thunder storm approach.

The big ones usually arrived from the northwest, pushing a few signalling gusts of wind ahead of them even before there were any clouds in the sky. One moment there would be nothing but the wire-buzz of July heat, then came a new sound and unpredictable movements. The leaves of just one tree would suddenly turn in unison, all touched by an invisible breath of foreign air that came puffing across the landscape, ruffling things here and there as if in warning. If I was at home when this happened, Mother's first move was to close all windows and doors in the house, no matter how hot the day or how far away the sounds of the storm.

"It's not here yet," I would plead, but that didn't matter. Lightning, my mother was convinced, could arrive far ahead of storms, as unseen as electricity itself, and it sought out openings in houses and struck as quickly as a snake for eggs. Even closing everything was not enough. Copper screens on windows, doors and porches were, my mother believed, an outright invitation to electrocution. So were chimneys, radiators, water pipes, light pull chains, bathroom fixtures, radios and switches of all sorts. Realistically, she knew these could not all be removed or disconnected for each summer storm, so they remained threats to our survival.

"We're in a valley here in Hancock," Mother would explain, brushing her hair back with the back of her hand and preparing to take up her position of maximum safety in the house—a straight-backed wooden chair placed in the middle of the front hall.

"Lightning always follows rivers and we're right between two of them." Unfortunately, like the plumbing, these two rivers could not be moved. They were, she said, the Charles River that flowed through Boston and the Blackstone River in Woonsocket, Rhode Island. Both being many miles from Hancock, I never really understood or even believed the River Valley Theory. Nevertheless, Mother clung to it and I knew better than to argue.

The first stirrings of a storm were usually followed by a new silence like the hushing of a well-behaved concert audience when the conductor taps his baton. At midday, under a full summer sun, there was a normal background sound in the woods and fields around the house, a dormant snoozing, a baking of the earth and everything on it. Bugs hissed and crackled. Cows stood up under trees, then lay down again, making distant noises with their bells and chains. Dogs thumped their tails at flies. Cicadas shrieked. But with the first smudging of the sky with oncoming clouds, all living things seemed to hold their breath and listen for the footsteps of the storm.

I used to like to watch the approach of this eclipselike darkness from somewhere outside the house, but Mother always pleaded not to be left alone inside, even though by then she was sitting squarely on the front hall chair, which she had calculated to be equidistant from all metal objects, fireplaces, bay windows or other threats of electric death.

When the sky turned blue-gray, then blue-black, the leaves of all the trees would appear silver and flutter strangely, turning up their lighter-colored undersides like fish rolling over before death. Then a few giant rain drops would come knocking here and there, propelled at random ahead of the wind, splotching down on still-hot pavements, not forming any pattern yet, just landing like the first mortar shells before a major attack.

When the black sky couldn't get blacker and turned green and revealed clouds within clouds that moved like I pictured intestines moving, then I knew it would only be a moment or two before the first stupefying arc of electricity leaped from sky to earth. If I was on the porch of the Winter house, it was like being on the bridge of a ship at sea and I loved it. But if I was at my house with Mother, such a storm was terrifying. I didn't understand why, but it was true and it gave me one more reason for thinking I'd be better off some-place else.

W HEN I finally got around to mentioning the subject of running away to Artie, I just came right out with it and asked him: "You ever thought about running away from home?"

His expression never changed and he didn't squinch or anything, he just said he wouldn't have time to run away because there was too much work to do on the farm. I thought maybe Artie hadn't understood the question, but when I asked it again and got the same answer, I could see that what Artie didn't understand was running away itself. He didn't understand that you had to have more than time to run away, you had to have reasons.

"Wouldn't you like to see other places besides this town?" I asked him. We were walking along the wall between his place and mine, Artie on his side, me on mine. We were picking up stones that had fallen during the winter and trying to put them back securely so they wouldn't tumble again. Artie's father said this job must be done each spring. Artie was much better at it than I. When he reached for a fallen stone with his long arms it was like a monkey scooping up a coconut.

"Wouldn't you like to just *see* New York City?"

"Oh, yeah, I guess," said Artie, as if the idea amused him. "Sure. I'd like to see all them places, but there's no point in wishin' for what ain't goin' to be."

"You could make it be, Artie," I said and I wanted to add that *we* could make it be, him and me, but I stopped short of saying that yet.

Artie didn't answer, he just turned one of the stones this way and that three or four times until it fit the top of the wall in a way that suited him. When the stone finally sat tight, he smiled.

"Can't you just *imagine* what New York must be like?" I asked.

A smiling silence.

I finally decided that *that* was Artie's problem—he didn't *imagine.* Artie saw only what he looked at and he only looked at what he saw.

For example, one day I decided to show Artie a favorite magic trick called the Siberian Transport Chain which I had bought by mail for 75 cents from the S. S. Adams Company in Asbury Park, New Jersey. It was really a sort of test, only Artie didn't know it. I wanted to see how he would react to my mystic powers!

There was a whole long story you were supposed to tell your audience while you were getting ready, about prisoners being sent to Siberia and having their wrists chained together and locked. *But,* I would explain, there was one prisoner who was smarter than the rest and he had figured out a way to escape from the chain . . .

"And I, ladies and gentlemen, now possess his secret! Please observe how my assistant is placing this solid steel chain around my wrists." (My assistant was always pretty and petite, wearing a very short skirt and a tight bodice and her breasts, at least the part you could see, were like two per-

fectly rounded scoops of the creamiest vanilla ice cream.)

Artie looked at the chain and the small padlock and he never changed his expression while I explained what was going to happen. It was not a look of surprise or of wonder or of skepticism. He seemed only faintly amused. I wanted him to be amazed.

"Go ahead now, snap the lock. See? I'm chained up, aren't I?"

"Yo're chained up all right," he said, smiling.

I was giving this performance in my mother's garage where we used to hang around sometimes, where she kept the 1928 Hudson and where all my father's old Massachusetts number plates were nailed up above the windows, all the years from 1913. I kept a lot of my stuff there too, including my punching bag and the full-scale model of a Thompson submachine gun I'd made in woodworking shop at school.

"Now I'm going to escape," I said, trying to make Artie's expression change. I paused. "Do you think I can?"

"S'pose so," said Artie.

I thought maybe action would speak louder than words, so I wheeled around like the instructions said you should (on a stage) and I turned my back (to the audience in the theatre) and I did what I had to do to get the chain off my wrists (which is easy if you practice a little) and then, in one flourishing motion, I turned around to face Artie, holding the loop of Siberian Transport Chain dramatically between two fingers.

Artie nodded. "Good trick," he said, still smiling faintly.

I wanted him to be stunned. He wasn't. I wanted him to ask how it was done. He didn't. In fact, it didn't seem he cared. And this was discouraging for a good many reasons.

The only thing that Artie and I really seemed to have in common was baseball. I was a Red Sox fan. When summer came, I always listened to the games on the radio, always the Red Sox, never the National League Bees. I knew the Sox roster and lineup as well as Manager Joe Cronin, including every player's batting average. It was a time in the American League when, for a number of seasons, the Red Sox were always finishing several places back of the hated New York Yankees. I couldn't understand this, for what greater collection of heroes could possibly be assembled than Lefty Grove, Doc Cramer, Jimmy Foxx, Roy Johnson, Rick Ferrell and Bill Werber?

When Artie came over to my yard to play ball, I'd talk about the Red Sox and he'd stand up for his favorite team, the St. Louis Browns. How anyone could be serious about such a team was beyond me, because the Browns were almost always behind the Red Sox and entirely unworthy of any intelligent person's interest. But Artie just didn't seem to care.

Whenever Artie had some time to play baseball, we had a sort of ritual sequence of events. It began with pitching, first one of us throwing hard and the other hunkering down to make a target like a catcher. Artie could toss a baseball very hard with those long arms of his. Over a two-year period he had registered 480 strikeouts.

Then we'd switch and Artie would be catcher. I regarded myself as a smart, cagey pitcher, none of this windmill stuff with the windup, but no matter how I threw the ball, I knew I couldn't make it curve.

("Did it that time?")

("Nah.")

My unofficial strikeout total was much lower than Artie's, but I almost never walked a batter. When I did, a gasp of shocked disbelief would come from the stands.

After pitching, there were fly balls and finally some batting practice, which usually didn't work out too well because our fungo hits just arched off into the weeds with no one out there to catch them. (Artie and I were about even in home runs.) Sometimes the ball was truly lost and since it was the only one we had, there was no choice but to kick through the fields until the grass-stained sphere with the frayed red stitching was found again.

"You ever been to Fenway Park?" Artie asked one day while we were searching for the ball.

"Oh, sure," I said, "lots of times." It was a lie. I'd been to Boston a few times, but never to a baseball game. My mother would have been quick to say, of course, that I had been to bullfights in Madrid and car races in Monte Carlo, but I didn't want to have to explain that to Artie. Besides, I wasn't sure how much Mother said about her travels was true.

"When you were at Fenway," Artie asked, "did you get a good look at that left field wall?" The left field wall was the most unique architectural feature of the Boston ballpark. It was the shortest in the majors and on some days, two-base hits rattled off its green, metal-clad surface like hail in a summer storm.

"Oh, sure," I said. "I've seen it. Some wall."

"Ever seen anyone hit one over it?"

"Yeah, lots of times."

"Must be great. I never been."

I felt more sorry for Artie who had never seen Fenway Park than I felt for myself who hadn't seen it either. Somehow, I felt that I *had* seen that left field wall. And, besides, I would really be seeing it someday soon, just as quick as I could make all my plans.

"You ought to go," I said to Artie. "That wall is something. Those Sox outfielders sure know how to play the caroms off it, too."

"Yeah, I guess."

We scuffed through the field together, swinging our feet like scythes, laying over the young grass, looking for the ball.

"How come they have that wall there anyway?" Artie asked.

I had an answer, even if I hadn't been to Fenway. Anyone who listened to enough games on the radio knew about Landsdowne Street where all the cheap home runs landed when they cleared the wall.

"Because of Landsdowne Street," I said.

"Oh," said Artie just as we found our ball.

.... *15*

IT was hot on Decoration Day, as usual. By May 30, 1936, summer was truly arriving, school would soon be over and the worst part about living in Hancock would begin: vacation.

Mr. LeBlanc's landscaping work was finished and new grass was up in the new South Promenade that he had laid out, also along the new Avenue Français, which branched off from the old Peony Path and was bordered with rows of spirea and barberry.

Hay had already been mowed on the farms nearby, putting the sweet green perfume of early summer into the air. From our porch I could hear the sound of horse-drawn mowing machines in distant fields, a rachety tick-ticking that was interrupted now and then by the farmer's faint commands to his horse. It could have been the sounds of field artillery on maneuvers, I imagined, unseen soldiers moving field pieces through old forests in Europe, getting ready for the war that Lowell Thomas said was coming.

In Hancock, people called Memorial Day "Decoration Day," the day flowers were brought to the graves in the Union Street Cemetery and the veterans of World War I and the Spanish-American War paraded in their uniforms, carrying old rifles on their shoulders at pitchfork angles.

My father had been too old for World War I, so he had never been a soldier. I imagined, however, that given the chance, he would have been a good one because he was such a good shot. He was buried in the family plot at the cemetery with other generations of his relatives. He had died when I was an infant, a fifty-five-year-old man most people had called Ned, but who Mother had always called Mister Barnard, or so she said.

I knew one thing about Father that she never mentioned: he had been married twice before he met her, but he'd had only one child, and that was me. Then he lived just long enough to bounce me on his knee a few times. I felt a boyish poignancy about that—sad for him, sad for me.

All I knew about Father, or almost all, came from Mother. Depending on her mood, she offered differing views of her late husband, and she passed all of these along to me at various times without regard for contradictions. Sometimes she said he had been a very sick man and should be forgiven for some of the terrible-tempered things he had done. Sometimes she said he was selfish and spent a small fortune on himself and all his fancy guns and automobiles. Sometimes she said her husband had been a witty, jolly man, especially with money in his pocket, which was quarterly, when the dividend check from American Telephone arrived.

To illustrate her late husband's sense of humor, she told stories she said he had told, none of which seemed funny to me, not even the one she repeated most often, about the time Father asked a waiter for a "drytini martale." Mother sometimes cried when she laughed. I couldn't stand that.

Decoration Day always seemed to bring the stories out, like official ornaments of the occasion, as if Mother felt, dutifully, that it was the appropriate time to freshen my memory of Father. Decoration Day also meant the annual trip to the grave to bring flowers and see that the grass had been properly cut on the plot.

"When we traveled abroad," Mother would invariably announce, "I never missed a Decoration Day. No matter where we were, I always sent a cable to Mr. Cox and had him place a wreath on the grave." To me, this sounded like something done for unknown soldiers.

Les Cox, one of Father's best friends, was the undertaker who had embalmed my father's body, dressed it in a tuxedo, attached the gold cufflinks and closed the coffin. He was also the person who had acquired my father's guns (in trade for the burial costs, I wondered?). Of course, Les Cox and Ned Barnard had been hunting pals and I supposed it was only natural that Les should get Ned's guns; but all the same, I often thought about those wonderful, double-barreled beauties and wished I had just one for my own.

"What kind of guns did Father have?" I would ask my mother, but she never seemed to know.

"All I know is, they were expensive!" she would reply. "One came from England, I think."

"Was it a Purdy?"

"I wouldn't know one name from another," she said.

Each year, on the morning of Decoration Day, Only Mother would ask Only Child to cut some flowers for Late Father. "Just things from the place, son, they're best," she'd say. They were also the cheapest, considering the Depression. No more fancy wreaths for my unknown soldier. Purple and white iris, the common variety, and white spirea from the hedge, and if the season was right there would be lilacs, too. Plus lilies of the valley, of course, don't forget them, Charles; he always liked them. This combination made what

I thought was a cold and mournful bouquet, bloodless, waxy-white and stiff. But it was the traditional assortment, it didn't cost anything, and since Mother seemed to feel it was somehow blessed for having grown from the very soil Father had once called home, I accepted the custom without saying anything.

Next year, I thought, when I'm not here, perhaps I shall send a cable from somewhere and have a wreath put on the grave again. I could see it. It would have a wide gold ribbon across the center with the words "From Your Son."

Other essentials for the annual expedition to Union Street were a small trowel, a mayonnaise jar (with the label removed) to hold the flowers, and the grass shears in case the cemetery people hadn't trimmed around the tombstone. "Your father paid for perpetual care on that lot," Mother would say, "but they don't even fill in with fresh dirt when the coffins settle." She was preoccupied with the idea that sunken spots in the plot were obscene telltales of what was going on below ground.

The grave was easy to find. It was marked with a large, gray stone bigger and newer than the small slate markers all leaning this way and that in the oldest corner of the cemetery. "Your father had the granite stone put in," Mother would sniff each year as we stepped onto the plot, "but he never asked me a thing about it." We would then inspect the area for any signs of coffin settling and all the names and dates engraved were reconfirmed as correct and explained again and the mayonnaise jar containing the iris and spirea and lilacs was adjusted one last time at the base of the monument before Mother and Son walked away from Father for another year.

Before going home in the Hudson, we always walked

around the cemetery. Mother would smile sadly and say hello in a hushed voice to people she knew. Decoration Day was a social occasion of sorts. Sometimes I wasn't sure whether she was referring to the living or the dead when she mentioned people's names as we walked along the rows of gravestones. "There's Mr. Pond," Mother would say and the remark might mean that a person she had known years ago was now buried at our feet—or approaching us on one of the cemetery paths.

"There's Auntie Brown!"

Auntie Brown was a large marble monument with an angel on top.

"You remember Auntie Brown, don't you Charles?"

"Wasn't she the lady with all the cats?"

"Oh, you do remember her! She'd be so pleased."

I remembered that I didn't like her and didn't like having to call her Auntie, which she wasn't, and particularly didn't like having to kiss her powdered cheek.

I also remembered showing her the Siberian Transport Chain trick and how she almost fainted when I snapped the lock on her wrists. Now I noted with a small satisfaction that Auntie Brown had settled somewhat in her plot.

I was always glad when the annual ordeal of Union Street was over, but never more than this year, 1936, which I was certain would be my last. "Union Street" meant death, a place full of Former People who weren't going anywhere (and who had not *been* anywhere either according to Mother) and who would now never escape the weight of earth that kept settling them deeper into their pits of perpetual care.

Mother used the words Union Street as a code meaning the

end, a convenient evasion of the word death.

"If you want to put me on Union Street," she'd say when she was angry, "then just keep it up!"

For me, there was always a particular reason to hope that the ceremonies and the ritual walk-around would not take too long, because the Indianapolis 500 was on radio and to hear this race described over the sounds of the roaring cars was one of the year's biggest thrills. Just as I knew the names of all the Red Sox players, I also knew the heroes of the famous Brickyard—Ted Horn, Rex Mays, Louis Meyer, Mauri Rose! Gladiators in cloth helmets!

There was a song the band always played before the race, "Back Home Again in Indiana," and then came the famous words, "Gentlemen, start your engines!" I had promised myself that some day I would be there and see it all.

.... *16*

I THOUGHT no one would ever catch me inside the
Winter house. It was shut tight and, from the outside, looked
more and more abandoned as the grass grew higher around
it. I supposed most people had just forgotten about the old
man by the time summer arrived. If he had any relatives,
they must have been hard to find.

I thought I left no track in the grass as I came and went
from the place and was careful not to let anyone see me when
I ducked around the north side of the house to go in the open
cellar door. All the same, after I'd been in the house a dozen
times or more, a day came when the place ceased to be my
own private hideout.

I knew that I'd been discovered when I heard footsteps on
the cellar stairs. I was sitting at the kitchen table, sorting
through an old box full of brass buttons and hooks and pieces
of chain and wondering if some of it might be gold, when I
heard the voice behind the door at the top of the stairs. "I
know you're in here, I saw you come in!" I recognized the
Wendell girl's laugh, deeper than her voice. I've-caught-you,
the laugh seemed to say. You thought you could hide, but
I've caught you in your secret place!

At first, I didn't know what to do. If I just kept quiet,

would she go away? Before I could make a decision, the doorknob turned and Annie Wendell stepped into the kitchen.

"You live here now?" she said mischievously, swinging both her arms around in a circle. "You like this better than your own house or something?"

She was joking, I thought, but I was uncomfortable. She didn't seem to mind that I had no business trespassing, she just seemed to think it was funny for the two of us to be there. I put the cover back on the box of trinkets, hoping she wouldn't think I'd been stealing stuff. The whole room was tinted green from the sun shining through the old window shade, and now there seemed a lack of oxygen. I could smell her perfume.

"Nobody's meant to be here," I said. "I was just poking around." I tried to make it sound casual, but I still felt like I'd been caught doing something wrong.

"You mean you're just here for fun?" she said. "You're not robbing the place?" I laughed, weakly, not feeling at all sure of myself.

"He might have had some money hidden, you know," she said, twirling around in the middle of the kitchen, as if she was at a dance. "Have you looked in all the closets and teapots?"

I had, of course, but I didn't want to admit it. I didn't know whether her curiosity was innocent or shrewd.

"This is the kind of place where they always find money," she persisted. "Old guys like him are sometimes even millionaires." She smiled at me, as if to say, wouldn't it be fun if we could find some money here? Was she suggesting that *we* would do something with it if we did?

"Are you going to show me around, now that I've come calling?" she teased.

I said I would, but there wasn't really much to see.

"Any beer in the Frigidaire?"

"No Frigidaire," I said.

Shit she said with a shrug. I'd never heard the word spoken by a female before. She confused me, disturbed me.

"The least you could do for a girl who comes calling is have a cold beer!" she said. I supposed she was still teasing, but she also sounded like she meant it.

"This is the kitchen," I said, lamely, trying to change the subject.

"How can you tell?" she said, looking around the room and laughing.

"Still a lot of cans in the cabinets," I said. "Mostly milk."

"You won't get anywhere with me with milk!" she said archly. "You sure there's no beer?"

If I could only get some somewhere, I thought. But I wasn't old enough to buy it and there was never any in our refrigerator.

"You come here often?" she asked.

"Only once or twice," I lied cautiously, watching her reaction.

"What's in there?" she said, looking through the door into the next room.

"A parlor and a bedroom," I said.

"Woo! Woo! Has it got a bed?" she asked. Again the deep laugh.

I let her see for herself.

"Aren't you going to give me a tour?" she said. "Or do I have to find my own way around this place?"

I followed her into the next room.

"What a mess!" she said, looking at the mountains of junk. "What makes you want to come here? This is awful!"

"It's a place to be alone," I explained hastily. "It's private."

"Isn't it more fun when I'm here?" she asked coyly.

I said sure.

She was persistent, almost annoying. "What I mean is, you don't like doing *everything* alone, do you?"

"It's okay," I said.

"You're a funny one," she said. "You think you're too good for everybody else, or something? Is that what your mother told you?"

"No," I said. "It's just that there aren't many kids around."

"I'm around," she said, sounding suddenly serious. "It's lonely for me on Maple Street too, you know."

I didn't answer; I couldn't think of what to say.

"Next time," she said, "you bring some beer—and I'll bring me."

I knew I could pretend I didn't hear what she was saying or what she might mean by "next time." But that would be admitting I was just a kid.

"What goes on at that school of yours anyway?" she said. "You guys all pansies or something?"

I felt trapped by the conversation. "We better get out of here," I said. "Someone may have seen you come in."

"Something first," she said, moving squarely in front of me like a challenge, her face turned up to mine. I could smell the perfume now, stronger, and could see the dark outline of her bra. Then she stepped closer and I could feel her breasts through my shirt. I felt like a dope. Was she doing this because I should have done something myself by now? Everything seemed backwards.

She lowered her voice and put her arms around behind my back. "How would you like to try kissing a public school girl?" she said, mocking. "Or wouldn't your mother approve?"

There was no point in answering. She was making it a matter of her or my mother. I felt the blood pounding up the sides of my head, making my scalp itch. I leaned forward, focused my eyes on her lips and saw her mouth open as it disappeared below my nose. I'd seen clinches in the movies, but I forgot to do anything with my arms which just hung at my sides. All at once I felt the girl pull back and toss her head. A wave of perfume rose between us.

"Come on!" she said, irritated. "Don't kiss me like a fish!" Open your mouth—or don't they *do* that in private school?"

I tried again. Her tongue passed between my teeth and slithered into my mouth. The invasion of my inner body felt strange. I supposed I should do the same to Annie Wendell, do it back to her if I could, so when her tongue was no longer in the way, I followed it back into her mouth with my own.

The stabbing pain was a stunning surprise, my eyes filled with tears and blurred. I raised my hands to her shoulders and shoved against her, but that only made the pain worse. My tongue was caught in a strong, steady bite, not just a quick accidental snap of the teeth, but a clamping hold, like a spring trap. The kiss had suddenly become a sadistic tease and the laughter in her eyes told me she meant to hurt. She was looking straight at me, her eyes only inches from mine. She spoke through her parted lips without loosening her bite: "Next time, say please!" Then she let go and laughed.

"Why'd you do that?" I asked, wiping my mouth with the back of my hand and looking for traces of blood. I felt slapped, rebuked, humiliated.

"Annie has to go home now, little boy," she said and skipped from the room and around the corner into the kitchen. I heard her sandals slapping the cellar stairs as she ran out the way she had come.

My tongue hurt, but not as much as my pride. True, I had thought about her, thought things about her, but she didn't know that. Or had she guessed? Was she punishing me for my thoughts?

When I got home, I didn't feel like talking, didn't want supper, didn't even listen to Lowell Thomas. The closeness of the girl was still whirling through my head. I felt like a fool.

Mother was fixing mackerel again. I watched her holding it up by the tail the way she always did before lowering it into the frying pan. Next would come the sputtering and the smell.

"Any news about Mr. Winter's relatives?" I asked, trying to sound as casual as my tight throat would permit.

"We'll probably never hear a word," she said.

"There must be somebody who belongs to him, don't you think?"

"Not necessarily," she said, turning her head to the side to avoid the spatter of the frying. "Some old families just die out that way. They come to an end."

•••••••••••••••••••• *17*

CONNIE JACKSON of Jackson Motors always wore a vest to match his suit, even in summer. I didn't know whether this was because he was an automobile salesman or because he was, as some said, a ladies' man. Whichever, the vest, along with fancy neckties and slicked-back hair, gave him a prosperous and citified appearance. I liked anyone who looked as if he or she might come from somewhere outside Hancock.

Connie Jackson and his brother Paul had been Dodge dealers as long as I could remember, even before Walter Chrysler came along and gobbled up Dodge into his new corporation. For some years after that, the story went, the independent Jacksons wouldn't have anything to do with such new corporate in-laws as Plymouth and Chrysler. Dodges had always been good enough for them and for their customers. Eventually, of course, they put up a new sign and parked some fancy new Chryslers behind the big showroom windows.

I had followed all this with interest. I didn't realy know anything about cars, but thought I should. According to Mother, the ownership of fine automobiles was a family tradition. "Your father bought a new Cadillac every year and went to the factory to select it," she would say as if telling me for the first time.

"Your father knew cars," she would tell me again. "Of course, he spent too much on them, but that was his way with many things." *Things,* I knew, also meant guns. I wondered what else. Had Father been a ladies' man too?

"If it hadn't been for my travels," Mother always said, "I would probably still be driving Cadillacs today." Then she would once more blame the Depression for our 1928 Hudson. The Hudson was a four-door brougham (Mother called it a "broom"), dark blue with a pair of spare wire wheels mounted in the front fenders. The windshield was a one-piece, straight-up type that could be hinged open to let the breeze in on summer days.

If asked, I would have said without hesitation that the Hudson was the dullest car in America. The most exciting? That was easy: it was the Chrysler Airflow—which, by coincidence, could now be seen at Jackson's garage. As far as I was concerned, the Airflow's radically streamlined shape (which some people were calling an upside down bathtub) was the most glamorous thing on wheels. Its split windshield swept back at a rakish angle, its hood dipped low like the front end of one of those fast European trains and the whole car looked as if it was going at least 50 when parked. Therefore, when J. Conrad Jackson, vest and all, drove up to our house in a golden Chrysler Airflow one Sunday afternoon and asked if Mother and I would like to take a ride, I suffered a spasm of joy that felt almost like fear.

"He wants to give us a demonstration!" Breathlessly, I brought the invitation to my mother in the kitchen while Jackson waited in the driveway, the engine of the Airflow murmuring power.

"Your father never liked Jackson," mother said, peeking

out the window at what she could see of the car. She wiped her hands on her apron, then untied the strings.

"C'mon, Mother, what difference does that make? Let's just take a ride," I said.

"He must have heard I was getting ready to trade," she said, smoothing her dress and arranging her hair. "Everybody *talks* so in this town," she added, but she didn't really sound displeased. I was pretty sure Mother wasn't really "getting ready to trade," but I didn't care. All I knew was that the car of the future was at this moment waiting in our driveway.

"Nice of you to come by," Mother said in her Other Voice as she came out onto the pee-azza. "I've been thinking of a new car," she lied gracefully, then added, "and I've heard about this Chrysler of yours." Jackson opened the car doors. I climbed in back, my mother in front. Jackson was going to drive, I was glad to see. Mother wouldn't have known how to manage anything so scientifically advanced, I was sure.

The realities of car salesmanship in 1936 required efforts such as "demonstrations." Most people, especially in Hancock, didn't go looking for a new car until the old one quit. New cars, even old established makes like Hudsons and Dodges and Packards, had to be brought around, all polished and shining, and hoods had to be raised and exhaust notes appraised for their connotations of power. Ultimately, of course, what was most important was the price. The less the better.

Jackson was full of pleasant talk as we drove up Maple Street and I guessed he was a ladies' man, whatever that really meant. When we arrived Uptown, he looked at Mother and said, "Well, where shall we go?" as if this great, graceful Airflow were capable of reaching any destination as effortlessly as an airplane.

"My husband always tested cars on Canning Factory Hill," Mother said—or was it "Cannon Factory Hill?" Even as she said it, I still could not be sure, *canning* or *cannon*. I never asked, however, because it wasn't important and Mother couldn't stand to have her pronunciation questioned. Nevertheless, I used to look at the old empty factory at the bottom of the hill and wonder whether they made cannons in there or cans.

Jackson laughed easily. "I remember that," he said. "People used to take cars over there to see if they could get all the way up in high gear." He added as politely as he could that, of course, all cars could now make it up the old hill with ease. Mother didn't answer; I knew she always shifted the Hudson into second gear on Canning/Cannon Factory Hill.

When we arrived at the test site in the Airflow it mounted the grade in one smooth surge, of course. I reclined against the upholstery of the rear seat as if I were in a royal carriage and let the power of the future press my body back into the mohair.

I had one stabbing thought as we cleared the crest of the hill: if Father were alive, he would probably buy this car today.

My thoughts wandered as Jackson took country roads I had never seen before. He turned on the radio; swing music bathed the sedan's interior with contemporary sophistication. The salesman explained the car's many new features as we rolled along, some of which he called revolutionary. I knew that kind of talk would get nowhere with Mother. The last thing in the world she was interested in was change.

"Well, this car may be all you say it is," Mother was saying, "but if you've traveled as I have, you know that the Europeans are still 'way ahead in automobile design."

I knew what was coming next. Jackson was either going

to get the story about the fast ride Mother had once had in a car called a Sunbeam or else it would be the story about what she called the "Hispano-Switzer" in which her "friends in Madrid" used to go summer touring.

I knew these tales by heart. Jackson listened politely to both, while cruising along roads that were by now far from the Territory. The Chrysler seemed more swift and elegant with each passing mile. Gradually, as easily as a silent shift of gears, the car became mine; Jean Harlow shared the front seat with me and we were headed toward the Glen Island Casino for a summer night of dancing under the stars. I wondered, would Jean Harlow wear the same white dress with the string straps over the shoulders? And would she kiss me like the Wendell girl?

As the enchanted afternoon grew longer and later, Jackson slowed the golden chariot at an intersection with what appeared to be a big highway. This was far enough he said; it was a good place to turn. I was totally lost by now, so confused in my directions that I might as well have been on a journey to Tibet with Lowell Thomas. I saw cars speeding along the highway in front of us, several lanes of automobiles moving in both directions. There were route signs with numbers and mileages and arrows pointing left and right.

Jackson was turning back now, but I wished—oh, *how* I wished—he might have gone onto that fine, fast highway and followed it no matter where it led! I had never seen such a road before or such an invitation. I stared out the rear window to take one last look at where we were *not* going—and then I saw the sign. In large letters, it explained everything:

NEW YORK 233 Miles

It could have been an electric shock, a bullet, a Joe Louis jab. New York! I could hardly believe what I saw. Just at the

97

other end of that ribbon of pavement, within reach of anyone who could simply *steer,* was the greatest city in the world.

By now the golden chariot was heading back toward Maple Street. Jean Harlow was gone; I didn't want her to see our house. I withdrew into my dreams. New York City was just next door.

18

IT was the last day of school for me, a Wednesday in early June. The next night there would be the dance and then graduation ceremonies for the seniors, but for day hops exams were over, locker keys had been turned in and another year was finished. There was a lot of silly horseplay around the Academy that day, kids saying goodbyes, making plans to meet in New York or Boston during the summer, talking about new cars they would have for their vacation trips.

One of the plainer girls asked me where I was going this summer, forgetting, no doubt, that inasmuch as day hops didn't come *from* any place, they would therefore have no place to *go.* Where-are-you-going-this-summer? was the question of the day being asked all over the campus without even thinking, so I just said I might be going up north to Maine. The girl, who had brown-brown hair and no shape at all and came from North Adams, Massachusetts, smiled and nodded and said she was going to England with her father and mother because her father's company was sending him to the London office.

I watched some of the boys holding hands with girls in sweet partings that the Academy rules about "touching" would never have allowed during the school year. The whole

99

scene gave me a pain. I hated those kids from Rye, New York, hated the way they pretended everything was so easy, oh *la de da,* wasn't it wonderful to have money? I also hated their private school—it was theirs, not mine—and most of all I hated to know that in a few days all of them would be somewhere else and I would still be here.

"It's your last day, you should look nice," Mother had said that morning.

"What difference does the last day make?" I felt like challenging all logic, particularly hers.

"Oh, I remember last days! It's always so sad and yet exciting to say goodbye to good friends." She was ironing my pongee shirt and I knew she was going to tell me to wear it because she thought it looked so nice with the red satin tie. I hated the pongee shirt, too, because it wasn't white or a color either, and made me sweat under the arms and left dark rings.

"I don't have any friends at school!" I announced. I wanted to add that I wouldn't wear that damned shirt either.

"Nonsense, son, of course you have friends!" she said, handing me the finished shirt, holding it up carefully by the collar. "Wear the red satin tie with it. That always looks so nice."

I couldn't wait for the last day to be over. When I got home, I yanked off the red satin tie without loosening the knot and pulled the pongee shirt over my hands without unbuttoning the cuffs. All I wanted for the rest of the afternoon—for the rest of the summer—was privacy. The best place to go was the Winter house, I thought. There would be something to do there, at least stuff to look at. I headed down the road.

Norm Claflin was out working in his garden. Though I

waved and said Hi, he only nodded. Mr. Claflin and his wife were in their forties, but they had no kids. They lived in a prefabricated house that Mr. Claflin had put together himself. It was an ugly little structure with a small front porch and a small front lawn surrounded on three sides by a dark stand of pines (which was where the Burly Stranger had come from).

I always thought it must have been quite a job for such a dried up little man as Mr. Claflin to build a house all by himself, even one that was put together from sections. But he'd done it. Mr. Claflin was a bookkeeper for a finance company.

Mr. Claflin's wife, Pearl, was almost twice as big as her husband, a large, well-rounded woman, not flabby fat, but always looking trim, full and healthy in her nurse's uniform. I could always hear things rubbing together when Mrs. Claflin walked by, as if she were forcibly encased in some unseen harness.

Pearl Claflin had reddish blonde hair, but didn't wear a nurse's cap because she wasn't really a graduate nurse. People called her a practical nurse. I wasn't too sure what that meant, but everyone in Hancock seemed to accept Pearl Claflin as a *nurse,* never mind where or whether she had gone to school. She knew the names of all the medicines and some of the things that went into prescriptions and she could take your blood pressure and give injections if she had to, even though Mother said she wasn't supposed to do that.

Although the Claflin house was more than a half mile down the road from ours, I thought of them as neighbors just the same. Mother had tried to get them to invest in some stocks once, but nothing came of it. "People like that never have money," she had said after she'd found out they didn't have money.

A couple of years before, there had been a big to-do about Pearl Claflin and a "burly stranger" who she said had broken in on her one night when her husband wasn't home. She'd already had some trouble with Doctor Lambert, the eye doctor. That time she said she had been molested during an examination. The burly stranger business was much worse though, because the man had come right into the house by pushing through a screen on the porch. There were a lot of stories about what happened then, but because grownups lowered their voices whenever they talked about it, I was never sure of the details. Apparently, Pearl was in the bedroom working at her sewing machine, looked up when she heard a noise and there he was standing in the doorway. Later she said she'd never seen the man before, didn't recognize him as anyone from Hancock. He was all out of breath, she said, and wet and covered with leaves from coming through the woods.

Everyone had talked about this for a long time afterward. Pearl wasn't hurt or anything. Mr. Claflin had just found her sprawled unconscious on the front lawn when he came home. She had come around pretty quick as soon as her husband spoke to her and she told how the man had torn at her clothes and how she had fainted. I thought this rather disappointing, but I knew it wasn't the kind of event on which to expect details. I guessed that Pearl probably remembered more than she wanted to say because most people called this incident a rape and it certainly was a first for the Territory. I didn't know whether rape was a federal crime or a state crime or both, but I guessed it wouldn't be anything important enough for Lowell Thomas to mention on the news— and he didn't.

There was an investigation, but the police never found the man Pearl described, so pretty soon The Rape wasn't even mentioned any more. Mr. Claflin went on working at the finance company and Pearl still went around in her nurse's outfit as usual and it didn't seem as if it could have been such a terrible thing after all.

I wondered about rape after that. I wasn't sure, but from reading the *American Weekly* I thought people who got raped were usually young, pretty women, who lived in New York apartments. Actually, if rape was a form of sex, which I supposed it was, I wondered where Pearl Claflin fit in. She was almost too old and she was so antiseptic looking in those uniforms.

Annie Wendell would be another matter I thought. If she got raped, it seemed to me it would be the real thing. Maybe that's how she got the kid. Maybe it was her own fault.

More than two months had passed now since the police had locked up the Winter house, with still no sign of any new owners. I hadn't been near the place much since the Wendell girl caught me, but on the last day of school I felt like looking around some more. All that old junk fascinated me. Also, now that I knew more about Mr. Winter and his job on the railroad, I understood some parts of his collection better. In addition to the umbrellas, books, eyeglasses, galoshes, hats, children's toys and other belongings that people had left on trains, there was a large pile of brown leather briefcases in a corner of the attic that I'd barely had time to examine so far. Most of these were empty, but some still had papers and other stuff inside. A few were stamped with their owners' initials. Winter's own Lost & Found. It didn't seem possible that passengers could leave so much stuff on trains, but then Conductor Winter had years to assemble his collection.

Now I decided to really search the briefcases. Some contained ancient copies of the *Boston Herald* and the old headlines and pictures made me think I was opening a time capsule. What else would I find?

Along with the briefcases, there were some old leather valises, black leather satchels, one carpet bag, several paperboard suitcases with straps, and one small black metal box with reinforced corners and brass hinges and hasps and the initials **NHRR** stenciled on its lid. More railroad loot, I thought, pulling the box into the watery light from the attic window so I could see if it was locked. There were only two snap clasps, which lifted easily. I opened the cover.

The money was right on top, in bundles, held together by rubber bands that heat and age had melted into narrow strands of brown glue. The bills were old and somehow didn't look exactly like the ones now in circulation, but they were genuine U.S. cash, I had no doubt about that, I knew real money when I saw it and that's what I was looking at, a whole conductor's case full.

The first handful I picked up was more money than I'd ever held before and I fumbled it like a deck of cards. Nervously, I returned these bills to the box without counting them. Under the money were stacks of old timetables, several packets of tickets and train checks and a nickle-plated conductor's punch, shiny as the day it was last used.

The noise downstairs might have been a squirrel, a woodpecker, the wind or a person. Quickly, I closed the cover on the box and held my breath. It was nothing I hoped, but I shoved the chest under the pile of briefcases anyway and waited in silence, sitting on the dusty attic floor, looking out the dirty window at the big pines behind the house. What if it was Annie again? Was she following me? I didn't breathe evenly, but in gulps, as if my lungs had to be instructed to inhale and exhale. I was frightened.

Money! On the last day of school . . . the first day of summer! The Running Away Summer! How much was it? Thousands? Yes, thousands, it had to be. There were several bundles, all tens maybe, and maybe more underneath.

The police notice nailed to the front door flashed through my mind. It was still there, it was the *law* and even though I didn't know exactly what it said, I knew it didn't permit any finders-keepers on the property. Trespassing or snitching old stuff out of the house might be passed off as kid stuff, but if someone took thousands of dollars, that was robbing.

I had to think. Running Away could suddenly happen tomorrow. But I wasn't ready, it was only the last day of school, no plans had been made, only lists. I decided to leave everything right where it was, for a day or two, what difference would it make? I didn't dare take a chance of being caught with the money. I knew I couldn't bring it home to count either. I couldn't be seen carrying a black conductor's case with NHRR on it up the street or even risk trying to stash it in our garage. The box had been hidden in Winter's attic for years already, so what difference would a few days more make as long as new owners didn't appear all of a sudden. A chance I'd have to take.

I sat perfectly still on the attic floor for minutes that were as long as a stopped clock until I was pretty sure there was no new sound in the house. Then I went downstairs, and downstairs again to the cellar, and out into sunshine.

On the way home my head was full of crazy thoughts. Like the day when the great train had stopped in Hancock station and I just happened to be there. What a coincidence that had been. I'd never mentioned the train to anybody because who'd have believed me?

And now this. I started to run up the street, but then I stopped in front of the Claflins.

What are you running for? I asked myself. You mustn't run now. What if Pearl Claflin saw you and wondered why you were running?

I slowed to a walk. There was plenty of time. It was still only June.

.... *19*

NOW I had to plan, I knew, I *really* had to plan. Being suddenly rich changed everything. I realized that if running away had been a sort of daydream before, it was now real. If I'd been kidding myself about doing this, all that cash was going to call my bluff. The money was going to *make* me do it. I was practically going to have to run away because there was no longer any excuse not to, not if I had any pride. What excuse would I have for *not* running away? The whole idea got big and scary, but I tried not to let it show in any way. In fact, I became much more polite and stopped complaining about mowing the lawn.

The absolute safest place to think about what I was going to have to do was at night, in bed, with the lights out. I was afraid all my thoughts were visible now, that somehow the money would be visible too. I needed a place where all the plans could be turned over in my mind without the risk of anything showing on the outside. Mother could never tolerate a facial expression that was not accounted for anyway. "What are you smiling about?" was one of her favorite and most threatening questions. Sometimes she said it when I wasn't even smiling.

The best way to make my escape plan, I thought, was to

107

concentrate on one aspect of the problem at a time. For example (once in bed) I'd try to figure out in my mind what was actually going to happen *after* I disappeared. How long would it be before the police started looking for me? Would they put out one of those sixteen-state alarms? And how long would it be before they quit looking for me? I must know that.

I thought about disguising myself, letting my hair grow, wearing sunglasses. And, of course, changing my name. I assumed there was enough money in the box to buy a car. Maybe, once I got out west, I'd be able to get one. I'd heard that farm kids could have driving licenses at fourteen in places like Montana, or was it Kansas? Anyway, a car would be a disguise. It would make me seem older, sixteen at least. I didn't worry about learning how to drive. I felt I knew already.

I daydreamed about driving up to a motor court in Indianapolis, parking the car and registering with my new name. Charles Hancock III? How would anyone know that this young man in the Chrysler Airflow had actually escaped from somewhere? It wasn't as if I'd escaped from jail or anything like that, I wouldn't have a guilty look on my face, just a regular grown-up one.

I'd have to be careful about the money, where I kept it at night and where I carried it. And I'd have to look out that I didn't spend too much in one place—that would arouse suspicions. But I could spend all I wanted to on food and Cokes and movies and baseball games at Comisky Park. I'd also buy a camera and get somebody to take my picture next to the Chrysler Airflow. Maybe a girl would take my picture. Maybe I would take hers. I thought about Miss Latham. "Can I come too?"

I knew there were going to be girls I would meet on the

road. I wasn't sure just where or how this would happen but there certainly were girls everywhere and with a nice new car and money I imagined that things would work out.

John the Barber always talked about how good it was when a young man had his first girl. *Had?* "Make you strong, boy. Make you fill out!" I could hear old John's words and feel the suggestive, pinching grip of his hand on my shoulder muscles. "Purifies the blood!" But John never said anything about how you went about the getting. "You *get* a nice girl, boy . . ." he'd say, but not *how.*

Actually, Running Away was easier to think about than girls. Won't it be great, I thought, when I can send postcards to some of the snotty kids at the Academy this fall? No return address, just the postmark and a few tantalizing words signed "The Day Hop," that town kid in the pongee shirt who nobody thought would ever go anywhere, who never went to the dances and couldn't smoke without coughing. "Hello from the Badlands of South Dakota," I imagined one card saying. Or "Written on a Mississippi River boat." Or "Greetings from Hollywood."

Also I'd have to guard my money or I'd get robbed for sure. Maybe I should take a gun for protection. A revolver. I knew where Mother kept my father's old pistol. It was all wrapped up in pink, oily paper and mothballs in a Louis Sherry candy box on the top shelf of her closet. She showed it to me once. She said she had thrown all the bullets away. Mother was afraid of guns.

Sometimes I wondered how she would take my disappearance, what she would say to all her telephone friends. I didn't think she'd be too upset. I considered whether to leave a note behind, but couldn't imagine what to say. Maybe just give her a list of the reasons. "Dear Mother," it would say. "I ran away because . . ." And then I'd put the reasons down, beginning with BECAUSE NOTHING EVER HAPPENS AROUND HERE and then the others in no particular order.

Mother would probably fold the note up neatly and put it with all the other stuff she kept, like my baby curls and baby shoes and all those letters I wrote to Santa Claus when I wanted the Lionel train. Mother stored all these sentimental trophies of my youth in the dining room sideboard, along with the souvenirs of her travels. In addition to the Spanish shawl, these consisted of a carved wooden bear, a sprig of dried white flowers and a miniature chalet from Switzerland (the chalet had pieces of mirror behind the windows and a music box inside). There were two dolls from Greece. One was either a soldier or a policeman in a white, pleated skirt and long white stockings. There was a box carved from Yugoslavian olive wood—and, for some reason, a little donkey cart from Sicily. This item always puzzled me because, so far as I knew, Mother had never been to Sicily. Nevertheless, when she showed people the donkey cart she always talked of spring mornings in Sicily and how colorful the carts were as they came down the country roads with their drivers all singing Italian songs.

The main thing to do with the souvenirs, of course, was to show them to "company" who came to visit, which was not very often but often enough. Mother used these treasures like exhibits for a lecture: a pair of small wooden shoes from Holland, a long-stemmed pipe from Tunisia ("All those people smoke opium, you know . . ."), the terra cotta bull from Spain, the toy tambourine from Capri (". . . that's where I learned to dance the Tarantella!").

It was a show I had seen performed over and over. By the time I was fourteen, it was embarrassing me to death and I always tried to leave before the ritual began. One by one, the

110

objects would be removed from the cabinet and withdrawn from their tissue paper wrappings until, eventually, all stood displayed on the dining room table while the guests made polite exclamations and listened to Mother tell her standard stories about camel rides in the Egyptian desert and the smooth-talking Italian con man who tried to sell her the Etruscan pottery and how the women of midlands England scrub their front steps with soapstone.

Mother's longest and most elaborate story was about crossing the Sahara Desert on a camel. I didn't remember doing this, but she always said I was there, right at her side, on a donkey.

The best of the souvenirs was always saved for last, of course, the beautiful hushed moment when the Spanish shawl came out of the Jordan Marsh box, its folds of black silk slipping away to reveal the colorful embroidery and long, dancing fringe. Sometimes I thought I could see my mother's eyes glisten with emotion as she twirled the shawl around her shoulders and announced her anxiously awaited declaration: Yes, Spain was *the* most romantic country of all! By then the guests always seemed ready to agree that Spain must be lovely and world travel must be a wonderful experience and wasn't Mother lucky to have seen all those places and to have so many nice things to remember them by?

That was the benediction Mother craved, an acknowledgment from Hancock folk that she was a special person. Then there was the polite, nervous retreat toward the front door and the people were soon gone, leaving all the souvenirs to be re-wrapped in tissue and put away once again.

Because its appearance was always saved until last, like the magician's most astounding trick, I grew up attaching the greatest importance to the Spanish shawl. I had seen it taken reverently from its Jordan Marsh box so many times and was sure that if the house ever caught fire, the shawl, above all things, would be rescued first. It came as a huge shock, therefore, when Mother announced one day that the pressures of the Depression were going to force her to dispose of the shawl.

Dispose, I thought, meant that Mother was going to sell her favorite heirloom—but not quite. She was, she said, going to *raffle* it. "I have so many dear friends," she said, "and I know they'll all want to take a chance." Most of these dear friends had witnessed the ritual presentation of travel treasures in the dining room at one time or another and they surely remembered the climactic moment when the shawl appeared. Anyone who had been through that would appreciate what a treasure was now being offered for sale.

"At ten dollars a chance, how can they refuse?" she said. "I'm only going to offer it to people I think will appreciate such a thing." Then she started composing the letter that was to go to the select few. She spent quite a while writing various versions because it was a delicate thing to explain why it was necessary to exchange the shawl for money and she wanted to express herself just right.

Finally, she had what she thought were the appropriate words and read the letter out loud to me to see how it sounded. It said she had reluctantly come to the decision that inasmuch as the arthritis in her hip was getting worse and the shawl would therefore no longer be worn at balls and other occasions, it seemed better if another dear friend could now enjoy it. Then she explained that copies of the letter were going to only a very few of her closest dear friends— she didn't say how many. The mention of ten dollars came discreetly at the end.

112

I nodded solemnly when she was finished and said, yes, that was fine, although the whole thing seemed highly embarrassing and I didn't know my mother had arthritis in her hip.

"How many contributions do you expect to get, mother?"

"You mustn't call them contributions," she said. "They're *chances.* These people are taking a *chance* and there's nothing wrong in that. Capitalism is based on taking chances."

Then she took her old Christmas list from the box with the leftover cards and started addressing envelopes. Apparently quite a large number of people were going to be invited to take a chance.

.... *20*

IT wasn't long after Mother launched her raffle that she decided it was time for us to get together on one of our traditional summer rituals.

"Go get the big white basin," she said one day about the middle of June. "If we don't make the root beer now, it won't be ready for the Fourth."

This was one event that never lost its excitement for me, not even when I was fourteen and knew for sure that I'd soon be buying all the Coca-Cola I wanted in ballparks and gas stations across the country—real soda pop that hissed with captive, nose-tickling power when opened. The root beer we made each summer in the white basin in the kitchen didn't do that. It just wasn't as good as real Coke, but it was ours and we could afford it.

Sometimes the root beer we made was too sweet and often it was flat and there was always some sediment in the bottom of the old brown beer bottles we used, but the best part was the feeling of having triumphed over the big, slick company that charged a full five cents for a few swallows of manufactured pleasure. Mother had the cost of our home brew all worked out. "It comes to less than a cent a bottle if you do as I say and be careful when you take the caps off so they can be used again."

For 1¢ a bottle, you could really enjoy a root beer, even in the middle of a Depression.

So, the big white basin was brought up from the cellar every year (the geraniums from the front porch were kept in it during the winter), washed clean, and Mother would tell me again that it was the very basin in which she used to give me baths when I was an infant. "Can you believe that all of *you* once fit in there?" she'd say, drying the inside of the pan. I never knew how to answer that, so I usually said nothing.

The sugar went in first, a big mound of it, ten pounds or more, and then the almost black, syrupy extract poured from the square Hires bottle and then water and, finally, the yellow yeast cake dissolved in a cup of lukewarm water to make the mysterious, cloudy insemination that would give the root beer its fizz.

Mother always said it was my job to make the root beer since I drank most of it, but she was always there, stirring with the wooden spoon or smelling or testing the brown broth and only when she had washed each of the old beer bottles and was sure everything was right did she turn over the bottling operation—"man's work," she called it—to me. Up and down I would pump the long arm of the capping machine, pressing the shiny brass-colored caps onto the bottles, squeezing the old, used caps on as good as new and, finally, producing eighty bottles, all somewhat sticky on the outside from overflowing root beer, standing row on row.

I never told anybody about my part in making the root beer. I was afraid there was something sissy about enjoying doing things like that with your mother. Those times when I'd share a cold bottle with Artie after baseball, I'd just say we were temporarily out of Coca-Cola, but would he like some of "my mother's root beer." Once, when Artie held the bottle up to the light and asked what was floating around in the bottom, I said it was some of the secret herb flavoring she used and then, before I even knew what I was saying, I added, "Mother got the recipe in India."

"Oh," said Artie, tipping his bottle to let the cloudy yeast residue spill out onto the ground.

Now that it was nearly the end of June and I was suddenly richer than anybody I knew, I figured I'd better talk to Artie again about running away. There wasn't any reason for putting it off much longer, not with all that money waiting to be spent. This time, it wouldn't be just the *theory* of running away that I'd talk about, but really running away, actually doing it. I decided to tell him he could come with me if he wanted to. I thought I'd also have to tell him that I'd have some cash with me, not a lot, but enough for the two of us, enough for plenty of good eats, new sneakers, sunglasses, Good Humors, bus tickets and ballgames. I wouldn't say anything about actually having enough to buy a Chrysler Airflow or Artie would think I was crazy.

I realized that every time I'd considered Artie as my running away partner he'd flunked the test in some way, but it didn't do any good to go on wishing that I had a real brother to run away with. Artie was the only candidate and that was it. But what I still had to find out was whether all the time Artie and I had spent together doing nothing much except getting to know each other's batting stance and favorite teams was going to add up to a real friendship.

I carefully planned what I would say for one last try— about the ballgames we would go to and all the ice cream and hamburgers and French fries we'd eat and the double-feature movies we'd see and the long stretches of 60-mile-per-hour road we'd find. I still didn't think I'd better say anything about the Airflow, not yet.

It would have been a good plan, too, if something hadn't happened that more or less spoiled the whole idea. It took place near Airplane Pond one day just before the Fourth of July. Artie didn't know I was there too, and I didn't mean to watch him, but I had to lie still where I was or he would have known I'd seen him. Afterwards, I never could say what I'd seen, not ever, to anybody. Nor could I think of Artie as a Running Away Partner any more either.

He was sitting on the soft earth with his back up against the trunk of a tree rubbing his shoulder blades back and forth like a cat massaging itself. His long legs were stretched out in front of him and his feet, in his heavy shoes, were splayed out right and left, the heels digging into the leaf mold, first one and then the other, as if he was doing a little dance while sitting down.

Artie's head was tilted back, his eyes were closed, his mouth open and his breathing came the way it does when you run up a hill and are almost at the top. In between these big breaths, he made little uneven gasps as if the pain of running was really a pleasure and if he ever got to the top, he'd fall down in the green grass and explode with joy.

From where I was crouched, I could see his long arms hanging straight down from his shoulders to his bony elbows and his blue workshirt sleeves rolled up and his two bare forearms in the center of his lap.

Very slowly and carefully, I crawled forward so I could see more. When I had inched up a foot or so, making not a sound, I noticed that Artie's big brown hands, which could hide a whole baseball when he was winding up to pitch, were now sort of choked up on this large thing in his lap. They were sliding up and down on the pale, shiny shaft of flesh that rose like some fresh-skinned creature Artie was struggling to subdue.

When it was all over and Artie had left the pond, I told myself it wasn't so important after all, it was just what some kids called getting a rod on.

It seemed to change things, though I wasn't sure how.

············ *21*

FOURTH of July was supposed to be the beginning of summer, but it felt more like the middle, especially in 1936 when time in the Territory seemed to pass so slowly.

About seven in the morning George came to his front door, pointed his 12-gauge shotgun at the sky and fired a single, shattering blast. This, plus a few snickers and epithets that he directed at all *sum bitches* in general was his invariable observation of Independence Day.

I often wondered just what George was thinking when he pulled the trigger of that old gun. Was this his annual moment to play Minute Man? Was he firing the first shot of the Revolution—or maybe just blasting his anger at Mother's fifty-two-windows-and-seven-doors?

The Fourth was usually the only day during the entire year when George's shotgun was fired. The rest of the time it hung on the wall in the small room he called his den, its length cradled by two upturned deer's hooves from which the fur had long ago peeled like the bark from a dead tree.

George's den was furnished with a rolltop desk, a cot covered with several small pillows, an oak swivel chair, a picture of the barebreasted White Rock girl on the wall, some old Hercules Powder Company calendars and a braided rug on the floor. Dim and dusty as it was, I liked the little room because of its maleness. The shotgun was on the wall, the rifle with the octagon barrel stood in the corner with the umbrellas, and ammunition for both was kept in the back of a desk drawer. On the Fourth, George always waited to clean the shotgun until I came over later in the day to visit. The scent of the solvents and the gun oil were sweet and the smell inside the spent shotgun shell, when I put it to my nose, was nothing short of Lexington and Concord!

Mother allowed me some money each year to buy firecrackers. These were purchased a few days before the Fourth, just as soon as the fireworks stand was erected on a vacant lot Uptown. This temporary structure was a flimsy framework of raw lumber with a dirt floor, a canvas roof and sides, and an open front. It was run each year by the American Legion Post with men wearing Legion caps behind the counter. There was no nonsense in 1936 about a safe-and-sane Fourth—those World War I-type Legionnaires would sell any size explosive to any size kid as long as he or she had money.

I planned my fireworks purchases as shrewdly as I bought penny candy. This meant spending a certain amount for daytime noisemakers such as caps, torpedoes, cherry bombs and strings of Chinese firecrackers called lady fingers. Then something had to be reserved for a show at night: Roman candles, red flares, a skyrocket or two, conical fountains of colored fire, sparklers and something special like *Big Bertha* or *Vesuvius Erupts* for a grand finale—and it had better be pretty grand if I was to spend 50 cents on it!

Mother and George were the audience for my show. Darkness wasn't really complete until after 9 o'clock, but George usually appeared at the end of our pee-azza before nine, holding his cigarette cupped in a hand behind his back and snickering like a mischievous child when my mother remarked, as she always did, about being awakened at 7 A.M. "by some terrible noise."

Ada never crossed the street to our side, but always promised that she would watch my show from her front windows. Sometimes I made a program of events and gave her a copy. The ten or twelve spectacular acts would all be finished in less than ten minutes, alas, such was the American Legion profit margin and the speed of burning powder.

Ada's observation of the Fourth consisted of sticking a row of small American flags into the lawn in front of her house. These had come from graves at the Union Street Cemetery over many years of collecting, with the result that some had 48 stars and some had less. Nor were they all the same shade of red, white and blue.

Although she probably never came right out and told him, Mother didn't approve of George waking the neighborhood with his shotgun blast. She always referred to Maple Street as a residential street and thought it was a pity that some people insisted on pulling down property values by raising hens or running a sawmill. "After all," she would say, "this is not the Crossing." The Crossing was an area near the railroad tracks mostly populated by the local Italians and the term was synonymous with slum.

It was probably because of this personal zoning system that Mother tried to regulate the hours of my own noisemaking on the Fourth. Ten o'clock in the morning was early enough, she said, for children from good families to start making noise in the residential areas. She had a special term for her permission.

"You can go bang off now," she'd say.

At school, the kids used the same phrase to mean masturbate or "jerk off," and hearing these words come so easily from Mother's lips always gave me a shock.

With the exception of George's shotgun blast and my own personal pyrotechnic display, no other forms of celebration took place on Maple Street. There were, of course, fireworks outside the Territory. There was always a show at the golf club, which was located somewhere beyond Uptown, but we were not members, "and your father never wanted to join either, although he was asked often enough." Golf club members, Mother said, were socially ambitious *noovo* rich. Never traveled, any of them, she decreed.

When darkness was complete and my own brief extravaganza had turned from hissing, swooshing brilliance to sweet, lingering smoke, I knew just where to look over the southern tree line to see some of the golf club show. First there would be skyrockets that splashed the darkness with color, then long pauses during which, I imagined, the golf club members were watching ground displays. Then the rockets would go up again, more furiously than before. Sometimes Mother and I sat in the two wicker chairs on the screen porch and watched together. And sometimes we had a root beer.

Later, pinpoints of blue and crimson and silver fire could be seen far off, silent signals of other celebrations in other towns beyond Hancock.

Finally on the Fourth, there was the heat lightning. Mother called it "sheet lightning." She said it was brought on by the fireworks, something about nature's reaction to all the banging off. Flickering on the distant horizons, it marked the end of the Glorious Day.

July 4, 1936, was just the same as all the others, I thought, only worse. Inside, I felt embarrassed to be doing the same kid things I'd always done. But I was fourteen now. Actually, I had enough money put away to buy out the whole

American Legion fireworks stand. I'd had my tongue all the way into a girl's mouth. I could smoke without having my eyes water and Lord knows what I might do next. But nobody knew any of this.

Mother's wicker chair creaked as she rocked and the red eye of her Chesterfield glowed every few minutes while she puffed in the darkness. Soon she was reminiscing about what the Fourth was like when my father was alive.

"Oh, what grand times we had," she said, her voice coming out of the darkness.

Nothing ever changed, I thought, not even the stories about how things had changed.

22

MR. CLAFLIN'S pants never had a crease down the front; they hung flat, like Chinese pajamas, and swayed from side to side as he walked. I often wondered what was inside his pants, for, unlike his wife, no trace of leg or knee or buttock ever showed.

One day Mr. Claflin caught me looking at him that way and he must have known what I was thinking.

"You've got good strength, boy," he said. "You got it in the legs and shoulders, too. That's good. I've always been a lightweight, myself. My whole family was. My brother weighed less than me." I thought that must have been an extraordinary sight because Norman Claflin was just about as dried up as any man I'd ever seen.

One of the things that made Mr. Claflin seem even smaller and more wrinkled was his big, smoothly inflated wife. Pearl always looked as if she'd been pumped up with too much air so all her wrinkles were stretched out. I used to think that if you could find the valve on Pearl and let out a few pounds, she might shrink down to her husband's size and be as wrinkled and old looking as he.

"Pearl's strong," Mr. Claflin said, again as if he were reading my thoughts. We were standing in his vegetable garden, me holding a brown paper bag while he filled it with summer squash and beans and other things he had a surplus of. "She's a fine, healthy woman, always has been." I didn't know how to answer that; besides, Mr. Claflin seemed almost to be talking to himself.

"When Pearl and I were married, we weighed exactly the same," Mr. Claflin went on, pushing his way between rows of corn. I followed. "There wasn't a pound between us, not even a pound. We were the same age too, just five months difference. Well, that's the way it goes sometimes," he said, turning to look straight at me. "A man wears out first sometimes, other times it's the woman. People are all made different, boy, you can't tell who's going to go first.

"You know what I mean by that, don't you, boy?" I nodded. The bag was nearly full of vegetables now. I was anxious to leave. I knew how much Mother would appreciate a free load of fresh food. But Norman Claflin seemed to have something on his mind and I didn't know how to excuse myself.

"My brother was the same," he went on. "He was strong enough in the arms and legs right up to the day he died, but he'd lost his manhood years before. It just must have drained right out of him like it did me." I thought this might be like drawing off the contents of a barrel—you couldn't see how much was inside and you couldn't be sure by tapping on the outside. One day the barrel just begins to run slow at the spigot and you tilt it up to get a few more splashes and then it's done.

"The women folk don't have it so bad, if you know what I mean, boy. 'Course, there's always some form of female trouble at certain times, but then it's not so much a matter of strength. With us, that's all it is, strength. I guess the good Lord gives us a certain amount in the beginning and it's up to us to make it last."

I laughed at that—a polite laugh that I hoped would be a way to bring the conversation to an end. But Mr. Claflin didn't laugh. He was just standing at the end of the garden now, his search for surplus vegetables finished, except he still seemed to want to talk about his wife.

"She's always been such a good woman, Charles, and smart too. She taught herself all that medicine, every bit, and she knows her drugs and her anatomy as good as any doctor. I've heard doctors say so. None better than Pearl Claflin, they say, when it comes to taking care of a sick person . . .

"That's the hell of it, boy, she's always taken such good care of me and now I can't do a thing for her any more. She's going to wither up, that's a fact I'm afraid."

The story was getting to be a long one, and obscure too. It made me feel uncomfortable. But I put the bag of vegetables down in the weeds at the edge of the garden as a polite gesture. Whatever I had planned to do next would have to be put off because Mr. Claflin wasn't just making conversation now, he was holding onto me with an almost pleading tone.

"You remember the man she said come through the porch, that night?" I nodded. "Wasn't no man at all, never was such a person if you understand what I mean." I nodded again. Mr. Claflin's voice was lower now, more confidential.

"I'm going to tell you this because I know you're a good boy, Charles. You've always been all right with us and you've grown up just fine too, a credit to your ma. I think you'll understand that sometimes folks have a problem they just can't solve by themselves. They gotta have help and they don't know where to turn.

126

"Pearl's not well, boy. She's imagining these things all of a sudden. She thinks people are comin' after her. That's what she thought about the eye doctor too, although I didn't know about her condition then. Seemed it could have been true, him bein' so strange anyway. Now I don't know. I think maybe she just imagined it like the last time . . ."

"That's bad, Mr. Claflin," I said, knowing this wasn't enough to say about someone who might be going crazy, but hoping it would do. For a moment, the sympathetic remark seemed to change something. We started walking out of the garden, in the direction of the Claflin house.

"She's always had a soft spot for you, boy, ever since you were a little one. She took care of you once when your ma was sick if you remember. She always said, 'There's a good boy, a fine boy, he's going to grow up to be something.' "

We had reached the edge of the lawn in front of the house. I could see where a patch of new screen had been put into the porch. It made me remember all the commotion that night. If I could just keep walking now, across the lawn and out onto the road and not have to stop to listen any more. I hugged the bag of vegetables to my chest with both arms and said, "Thank you, Mr. Claflin . . ." But Claflin didn't hear me.

"You've got strength, boy," he said again, looking at my arms around the bag. "You've got it in the legs and shoulders, too. You've got the strength boy, the strength of youth. When you're young, you've got more strength than you need, we all do."

"I guess so, Mr. Claflin," I said, but I had made the mistake of stopping on the lawn. The little man stood in my way now, his empty pants hanging like wash on the line, his thin face wearing a look of fear.

"Pearl would like to see more of you some time, Charles,"

he said. "She said so. She said, 'Charles would be fine, he's a fine boy and he's someone we've known.' She meant that, boy, I know she did. She wouldn't pick just anyone . . ."

She wouldn't just pick anyone? I felt something tight around my head, almost a dizziness. "You mean she picked me for something, Mr. Claflin?" I managed to ask.

"I thought you'd understand, boy. I hoped you would. I didn't know how to tell you about Pearl. I was afraid to come right out and say, 'She picked you, boy.' It's not an easy thing for either of us, you know, not easy at all . . .

"You could have all the vegetables you want anytime," he went on, his expression changing, a small smile on his lips, as if something had been decided at last and there was a load off his mind.

"She picked me for what, Mr. Claflin?" This was a crazy dream. I knew the Claflins were poor, Mother had said they didn't have a thing. That must be it, they didn't have enough money for medical care, they couldn't afford some operation for Pearl's female trouble, there were bills to be paid, something to do with the struggle she'd had with the Burly Stranger. It was money that Mr. Claflin was talking about, wasn't it? Money that he thought I could get from Mother, maybe.

Then I thought about the money in Winter's attic and a dim, confused picture of the bundles flashed across my eyes like a vision, like something that might get me out of this endless conversation.

"If Pearl needs some money, Mr. Claflin . . ."

"Thank you, boy. You're a good boy and I'm sorry I said anything." The smile was gone from his face now, his voice was suddenly deeper and tired, he didn't look frightened any more. There was only a blank look in Mr. Claflin's eyes.

"I meant it about the money," I said. "I might be able to help you myself, but you'd have to keep it a secret."

"It's all right, boy," said Mr. Claflin. There was relief in his voice, the tension was gone. "You go home now. You go home. You're a good boy and we know that. She shouldn't have picked you. It was the wrong thing. You're not the one, you couldn't be."

"I hope she gets better, Mr. Claflin."

"It's all right, boy. Just don't say anything about all this. Come pick whatever vegetables you need any time. You don't have to say nothing to either of us."

MORE than a month had passed since I'd found the money, but I didn't go back to Winter's attic, not even to take a second look at the fortune I'd seen in the conductor's case. I didn't dare. I was afraid someone would see me or follow me, the way Annie Wendell had that day. Anyway, where could I put thousands of dollars so that they'd be safer than right where they had been hidden for years?

After a while, however, I did begin to think it might be all right to take just *some* of the money out of the attic, maybe half or less. At least I'd have that much for myself if Winter's relatives showed up and cleaned out everything. I didn't think the money should be any more theirs than mine since nobody knew who they were anyway—what if they were rich and didn't need it as badly as I did?

For example: If I'd just had a couple of extra dollars on the Fourth of July, I could have bought several more boxes of cherry bombs. Or I could have an egg *shumpoo* someday. Or I could give Mr. Claflin something for Pearl—and maybe a dollar or two for the bagpiper if he ever came back again. Or Ada. She could certainly use some money.

I wanted to include George too, but he'd only spend money on whiskey and I'd be responsible, in a way, if anything happened while he was drunk. So I wouldn't give anything to George, but I'd give some to his mother. She'd want to know where it came from, of course, but I'd just wink and maybe she wouldn't ask any more questions. She always winked at me when we were sharing a secret, like don't-tell-your-ma-about-the-raw-frankfurt. Maybe I could just add a ten dollar bill to Ada's secret money hidden behind the picture of the *USS Constitution* in the parlor.

The way I figured it, there was so much money in the attic, giving a little away wouldn't matter, especially if Artie or nobody else was going with me when the time came. Then the whole bundle would be mine and I certainly didn't need several thousand dollars to get away from Hancock, Massachusetts.

Oh, yes. I knew Mother could probably use some money too, but I didn't see any way I could give it to her without telling her the whole story of how I found it. And that would be impossible.

By the middle of July, all the heat of summer was accumulated in a huge blue glass bowl turned upside down over the Territory each day. You couldn't see it if you looked at the sky because it was transparent and so big that airplanes could fly around inside it, but the bowl was there just the same and it shut off all the breezes and magnified the rays of the sun.

The lawn stopped growing under the glass bowl and all Mother's new avenues and paddocks and promenades that Mr. LeBlanc had made began wilting and turning brown. Water in the well went lower and lower, and the electric pump made a dry gurgling sound. Escaping the heat was something that had to be planned every day. It even interfered with making plans for running away.

When it came to finding cool places, choices were limited. The cellar in Winter's house was always okay because it had a dirt floor and almost no light, but there was nothing to do there except maybe get caught. The woods were steamy and full of bugs now, especially around Airplane Pond. The cedar grove smelled like an oven in which pine needles were baking.

Actually, one of the best places to go in the middle of a hot afternoon was the apple orchard behind Ada's house. Any breeze at all seemed to come there and the shade was soft. That's where I was one Sunday in July, just sitting under the trees, reading the comics and eating a piece of cold pie, when George called from the barn door. He beckoned me with the gesture that meant come-here-and-come-quick.

Probably has something new to show me, I thought. Maybe a clever new hiding place for a whiskey bottle or a fishing lure made from a real dried-up bug or an old Massachusetts license plate or a switch-blade knife or a forked stick for finding water. With George, it could be anything and sometimes it was interesting.

I walked over to the barn, finishing my pie as I went, and followed George's gestures into the garage side where the Chevy was parked. Hay and dust from the loft had sifted down on the small car and given it a powdering that made it look even older than it was. However, what George was going to show me didn't seem to concern the car. From the look on his face, it was something he considered devilish.

"I saw you in the woods that day the plane crashed," he began. He had the same sly smile on his thin lips as he did when he revealed a hidden bottle.

"I watched you pick up some pieces," he went on. The crash had happened more than two years ago. I didn't really remember who was in the woods that day, it seemed like everybody in the Territory and half the town of Hancock was there and then some. George must have seen me pick up the hunk of crushed aluminum that I still kept.

"Lookee here," he said, nudging me in the ribs and pointing to the rear of the garage. "I bet you never saw anything like this before!"

Some animal hides hung from a joist. It was the usual collection, three or four skins turned inside out, their fat-lined insides dripping in the heat, bushy, black-and-white tails hanging below. There was a coon skin there, too, bigger than the skunks' and gray, like an old man's beard.

"Look at this one," said George. "Ever see one like this?" He laughed and the leaves rustled in his throat as he coughed up the cigarette tars. His small eyes were sliding back and forth between the row of skins and my face, waiting for me to recognize something.

The skin George had singled out had short hair and no layer of yellow fat. It was dark and looked like something that had been run over by a car and left to dry on the highway.

"Don't recognize it, do you?" said George, the sly smile spreading.

I stepped closer, still holding my rolled up Sunday comics.

"It's *him,*" said George.

"Who?"

"The pilot. It's his scalp." George's laugh was hoarse.

Now that he had told me, I could see it probably was human hair matted on dry flesh. Short, barbered hair that might once have been blond. Just for an instant I thought it could be my older brother, the pilot, the one who had gone away to flight school before we ever had a chance to become real pals.

"They didn't see me get it," George said. "It was in a bush, all by itself. By-jeez-Christ, he sure must have *scattered* some when he hit!"

"You going to keep that?" I asked.

"It's just a joke," George said, but the sly smile was fading now because he could see that I didn't think it was funny.

"Don't take it serious," he said. "It was just for a joke."

July 16, 1936
1) Ada is right, George must be going crazy from drink
2) Saw Annie with two boys in a car today, but she didn't see me
3) Winter's attic may not be safe much longer
4) If I ever die, I hope it won't be in an air crash.

24

THE bagpiper came down the road again one July evening. The faint cry of his music filtered through summer's dusk and with it I was sure I saw a company of Highlanders advancing bravely to rescue Only Child. (Only Child was being held in the ancestral castle because he was not yet old enough to claim his late father's land and titles.)

Mother and I were completing the required after-supper walk about the castle grounds, bringing water to the royal birdbath, looking for new buds and blossoms in the plantings, inspecting the French gardener's work. We surveyed the Paddock, a kidney-shaped gravel turnaround where the Hudson was sometimes washed (always with natural sponges and chamois because that was Father's way); the Peony Path, which was a route for processions of Lords and Ladies; Avenue Grandmama, bordered with phlox and iris; Boulevard Charles the Third, formed by spirea and forsythia (my father and grandfather were Charles I and II); from there to the Sunset Seat, a spoon-shaped stone throne that Mother had had built facing west for contemplating sunsets. No one ever sat in it, however, because it was cold and hard and birds used it as a toilet.

Mother gave no sign she heard the bagpipe music, even

though it was clear enough in my ears. Her ritual tour was finished and she headed for her usual sitting place, the wicker rocker behind the bronze-green protective curtain of the front porch screen. She always wanted me to sit with her on summer nights while she talked about Paris or the old days in Hancock or the prospects for Red Feather Mines. I always tried to think of an excuse not to.

Tonight I said there was something I had to do first.

"Now what could be so important that you have to do it right now?"

"It's nothing, Mother. It's just something . . ." Why didn't she hear the music, I wondered.

I ran-walked-ran through the gathering darkness, following the stone wall that paralleled the road, moving away from our house as quickly as I could. The long, reedy notes were coming closer. The street ahead was a tunnel through black trees. I could see the piper's shape ahead, that of a small man carrying an armful of sticks. When he was nearer, I saw he was wearing the same rough pants and heavy shoes he had worn in spring, but now he had no jacket or tie or hat, only a collarless shirt open at the neck.

"Didn't you say you knew my father?" Our paths had met in the hollow beyond our house. He let the music wail to a stop and slowed his steps.

"Hello, boy."

"Remember me? You said you knew my father."

"I knew him. You're from the big house yonder." He had stopped marching to his own music now and we walked along together.

"It has fifty-two windows and seven doors."

"How old are you, boy?"

I told him, wondering why he asked and what question would follow. I also wondered if Mother would hear our voices. We were walking slowly toward the house and she was on the porch.

"Your father's been gone a long time. It makes me feel old to think of him."

"You're not old."

"I am, but walking keeps me fit."

"Where do you walk from?"

"Not from Hancock. Beyond."

"And where do you go on this street? Do you know someone here?"

"Only you nowadays, boy!"

"Do you know my mother?"

"She's on the porch, isn't she?"

"Yes, that's where she sits."

"I only know of her."

"Do you need money?" I blurted it out. It was what I had wanted to ask him since April.

"It wouldn't make me any younger. And it wouldn't make the road shorter," he added. "But where would a lad like you be getting money to give away?"

"I didn't say I had any," I said quickly. "I just wondered if people pay you—if that's why you play the bagpipes."

"Why do you play baseball? I've seen you and the other boy playing baseball."

"For fun." I wondered when he had seen us.

"I suppose. I never played games when I was a boy."

"How did you happen to know my father?"

"I knew him the best way you can know another man. I worked for him. Here on the farm. When they'd bring all those fine, fancy horses out from Boston and put them in your barn, then your father would need extra help. I'd exercise the horses and curry them clean and muck out the stalls. I was a young lad then and he was a gentleman, not like most around here. He wore fine clothes, tweeds and worsteds; and sometimes in the afternoon, when my work was done, I'd pull traps for him right there by the barn."

"Pull traps?"

"Trap shooting, lad! There's a catapult machine that flings the clay pigeons off into the air and someone has to pull the release cord when the shooter calls 'pull!' "

"Did he always hit them?"

"Oh, lad, could that man hit them! Fifty straight he'd shoot some afternoons, just like clockwork: *pull, bang, pull, bang, pull, bang*! He handled a gun like it was a musical instrument, lightly in his hands, never rough, always graceful." The piper turned silent. Then, as we walked on, he cleared his throat and said, "Will you pardon my asking, but what do they say your father died of?"

I said I didn't know. "Why do you ask?"

"It's just hard to imagine him dying of anything, that man. He was a proper gentleman, he was."

It was dark now. I could feel the mass of the house near us on the edge of the road. There were no lights in the windows yet, which meant Mother was still on the porch. It was a good thing the piper had stopped playing, I thought. She would have certainly heard the music and come to the end of the porch to see what she could.

"I must be going on now," my friend said, adjusting the weight of the bagpipes on his shoulder.

"You won't have to walk much farther, will you?"

"It's a nice night, I like to walk."

"Will you come again and tell me other things?"

"I'll come again, the good Lord willing." I thought I heard him laugh softly, but I could no longer see his face. He was painted over by darkness.

"I hope you do," I said.

"Will you still be here?" he asked.

What did he mean? Why wouldn't I still be here? Could he know I was thinking about running away? I couldn't tell him about that. I couldn't tell anybody.

"I'll be here," I replied. "I'm always here."

25

....

"THAT Pearl's a crazy bitch," George said. "And Claflin must be crazy too."

Worldly wisdom was coming. When George used swear words, I knew it was going to be man talk. We were sitting at the edge of the fishing hole. George had a brown paper bag on the ground at his side and held it up to his face from time to time as if he were getting ready to blow it up with air like a balloon and then smash it, *bang!* Of course, I knew he wouldn't do that because I could hear the whiskey gurgling inside.

"Pearl Claflin must be goin' through the change," George said. "Crazy bitch. Always has been. She's no nurse, she couldn't cure a wart, that one!" He kept the tip of his black metal fishing rod moving up and down rhythmically. The worm on his hook was dead, I was sure, but I supposed the movement might fool something. To save worms, I did the same thing. Neither of us ever used a whole worm because George never brought enough of them. It wasn't the Depression, it was just that he was too lazy to dig them.

We didn't speak for a while, then George asked me to hold his pole while he lighted one of his roll-your-owns. Pearl

Claflin must have been still lingering in his mind, because after puffing for two or three minutes he said Crazy Bitch again, mostly to himself.

Only a little sunlight slanted into the space above the pond —the hole in the sky that had been made by the airplane— but the shade in the place wasn't cool. Since July, the level of the water had gone down several inches. George said it drove the fish deeper. I wondered if they went all the way down to the deepest part where the engine of the plane still was.

"Mr. Claflin told me that all those troubles of hers was just imagination." I was trying to contribute to the man talk. I was glad I had something I could say that George might consider news.

"All right for him to say that now. He knows the truth about her, but he still raised a ruckus every time she screamed rape."

"She wasn't, was she? Raped?" The word was hard to say.

"Hell, who'd want to try?" George's glance slid over onto me and he pulled his lips into such a grin that I could see his old teeth. I didn't answer, but he kept looking at me as if his last words were really a question requiring a reply of some sort. They hung in the still, hot air: *Who'd want to try?*

"You've got a bite!" I lied, pointing to the spot where his black fish line spiked down into the gray water. George reeled in his worm, which was limp on the end of the hook and had turned all white.

"I tell you what I think," said George, pulling the stuff off the hook. "I think she made all that trouble for herself. Nurses is strange, you know. They can play games that other women wouldn't dare, talkin' sweet to the menfolk, always kiddin' around about lift-your-shirt and drop-your-pants and that sort of thing. I'll bet she got fresh with someone once too often and she got what was comin'."

I wanted to change the subject. After all, George was fifty years older. I gave him one of Mother's Chesterfields. He liked them better than the Buglers he made for himself, although he didn't admit it. Giving him a cigarette was the price of smoking one myself.

"Gettin' to be a regular little chimney, ain't you?" George said as we both lighted our cigarettes off his match.

"Don't ever tell!" I said.

"I don't tell your ma nothing. She don't listen to me."

We fished and smoked. I thought of telling George about Mr. Claflin's proposition that day in the vegetable garden, how he'd picked me out for Pearl. Now that would really be something to tell, I thought, *whoooeee*! But then, if George had asked me to explain what it all meant, I didn't think I could and I sure didn't want to appear as dumb about such things as Artie.

I had also thought of telling George about running away, at least about the idea, not that I was actually going to do it on a certain day or anything definite like that. But then I thought better of it because he couldn't help and he'd only tell Ada.

The pond was silent. Water spiders did a dance on the surface. It seemed we had run out of things to say until George spoke up without taking his eyes off the end of his pole.

"Ain't no shortage of pussy around here anyway," he said. "No reason for anyone to come after Pearl Claflin and get in trouble about it. You'll see, boy. Your days for sniffin' are all ahead of you. How about that Wendell girl? You tracked her yet?"

That was something I didn't like about George. He might be quite a fisherman and hunter and trapper and a sportsman

142

who owned several guns, but I was sure my father would never talk like that. And I knew he wouldn't drink whiskey out of a paperbag, either.

It seemed summer's required chores would never end. At breakfast every morning, Mother talked about which area of the Estate needed weeding next and how the rambler roses were falling off their trellis and should be pruned and why I should put more wood ashes along the lilac hedge where it was doing poorly.

The time between breakfast and lunch was the longest. There was no baseball game to listen to then, Artie was usually scraping hen manure for his father, Mother was on the phone with her stock customers and George seldom came out of the house to do anything, except go to the toilet in the barn, until afternoon. Sometimes I saw the Wendell girl, but she was usually with another boy.

By ten o'clock you could tell whether it was going to be a hot day or a *really* hot day, the kind that would bring a thunderstorm by 4 o'clock. I'd set a course around the Territory and do things to kill time. First I would give George's rabbits some vegetable tops to eat, then drop some bugs into the rain barrel where the two fish still lived. I'd search out new places to pick wild blackberries and maybe take a slice of bacon from the refrigerator and go put it on one of the ant colonies.

After the bacon fat turned from white to greasy gray, thousands of red ants would work on it from the edges. There would be so many of them after a while that I couldn't see what they were eating. The ants could usually finish off a slice in about twenty minutes.

Some mornings I'd practice with my Tom Mix lariat or work on a new magic trick. I wanted to show George the one where I pulled a lighted match out of my pocket. That would be good some time when we were smoking cigarettes together, I figured.

Frequently I let my thoughts wander off to Pearl Claflin. Just the nearness of her in the Territory intrigued me—maybe it was her notoriety. Sometimes she was just Pearl in my thoughts, not Mrs. Claflin. *Pearl.* Creamy white and opalescent. Round and smooth and young-motherly. A nurse who could make things all right again by rubbing on cool creams or healing salves, and wrapping wounds in clean white gauze. Sometimes it seemed she didn't really belong in Hancock at all, but was a sort of visiting angel standing by to help if disaster struck—and who had been struck herself while she waited. Who *was* the Burly Stranger, really? Would he strike again?

And then I'd find myself wondering what she must be like *underneath,* whether she was fat or trim, whether everything she wore was white. When I let myself think that way, I felt awful, but then I'd do it again. Mrs. Claflin must have been over forty.

I wondered if she affected other people this way too and if that's why those strange things had happened to her. If so, they'd probably happen again because I knew some women just had that sort of power and couldn't help it, couldn't control it. A magnetism, perhaps; a lure, like the stuff George put on traps. Maybe some women had more of this than others and that's why their own needs were greater. Maybe that was what Mr. Claflin had meant about Pearl.

I hadn't talked to Mr. Claflin again since that day in the vegetable garden; and whenever I saw him coming now, I disappeared. Mr. Claflin went by my house in his Willys every morning on his way to work. The car always left a trail of blue smoke. Sometimes Pearl was with him, looking like a daughter out for a ride in her father's old car; but when I didn't see her, I knew she was at home—just down the road.

No matter how bored I was, the one thing I didn't dare do was go back to Winter's attic and take out the money, not even some of it. But every day or so I'd stroll past the house, to make sure everything looked the same. Knowing that all that cash was in the attic was an awful feeling—like being responsible for a robbery that hadn't happened yet. I told myself I was just as guilty of stealing as if I had already taken the little black box out of the house.

One August afternoon when I was walking down the road, Pearl Claflin called to me. Her front porch was in deep shadow. I wouldn't have known she was there.

"Charles," the voice said. It sounded like a word that had floated away, no longer attached to the person who had spoken it. A big, round comic strip balloon containing only one word, *Charles*. I looked around. No one was in sight on the road, no cars, no breeze, just white sun heat coming straight down.

"Here, Charles," the voice said. "It's Pearl."

I looked at the house. Mr. Claflin had built it himself with the prefabricated parts that old man Navotny assembled and sold at his saw mill. These big slices of pre-built house were Navotny's own invention. They were already put together, eight feet high and four feet wide, shingles attached on the outside, plywood walls on the inside. You could buy solid sections or sections with windows already in them, or doors or whatever you wanted. You bolted the parts together and designed your own house. Some people said the only ones crazier than Navotny were those who bought his house parts. Navotny said such people would have another opinion shortly, once he got his production rolling, which he couldn't do yet because he was unable to get a patent on his invention because he was a foreigner.

"Up here on the porch," the voice said.

It was an awful looking house.

"Come in a minute, please, Charles, you can give me a hand with something."

I had stopped on the road. I knew now who was talking and where she was, but I still couldn't see her. I didn't want to see her. I was scared of the ideas I would get if I didn't think about something else, anything else but Pearl Claflin. So I studied the house, counted the windows and doors, thought about crazy Navotny, looked at the section of new screen at one end of the porch where the Burly Stranger had burst in.

"You scared of me or something?" she said, coming to the porch door. "I'll fix you a lemonade for the heat." Her voice was young and clear.

I left the road and crossed the lawn and came up the three steps to the porch while she held the screen door open for me. I think it was only then, on the top step, that I said hello. I didn't know what to call her. Mrs. Claflin or Pearl or what.

"My, you've grown to be a real young man, haven't you?" she said, taking a step back to measure me head to foot. She wasn't wearing her nurse uniform, just her usual white shoes and stockings with a summer dress that had flowers printed on it.

"Why don't you set yourself while I get us some lemonade," she said. "I don't think you've been to visit me since you were a boy and your ma sent you down here to be looked after while she went to Boston about her stocks and bonds."

I sat on one of the porch chairs and looked out at the road through the scrim of the wire and felt as though I had just stepped out of my own Territory into a shady cage. She had

146

been knitting. Balls of white yarn were in a basket near a chair, an unfinished white something was dropped on the floor. There were magazines and newspapers on a small table. Inside the house, I could hear ice falling into glasses.

"There now, tell me all about yourself." The glass she handed me was tall with white daisies on the outside and the lemonade had a sprig of mint leaves on top.

"Not much happening around here," I said, thinking of the money in Winter's house at the same time. I wondered if Mr. Claflin had ever told her I had offered them money if that's what they needed. Was that talk in the garden all just his idea, or was it true, like he said, *Pearl picked you, boy*?

"You won't be going away this summer, will you?"

"No, ma'am. Not right away, that is."

"You used to go to Maine when you were a little boy."

"I used to go to camp in Maine. But I can't any more."

"Well, you've seen more of the world than most young men your age around here. All that traveling with your ma must have been quite an experience." The Claflins had seen Mother's souvenirs, of course, had stood around the dining room table and passed the wooden shoes. Pearl had lifted up the Greek policeman's skirt to see if he wore shorts underneath and laughed when she saw he didn't.

"Do you still do magic tricks, Charles?"

It seemed she was trying to be nice to me, like she was getting ready to ask a favor.

"Oh, sure," I said as matter-of-factly as I could.

"You had a trick you did with a chain, remember? You showed it to me once at your mother's house. You put the chain around your wrists and told me to snap the lock and then you made one quick move and the chain was off."

I nodded and smiled self-consciously. The old Siberian Transport Chain amazed 'em every time, I thought! Of course, for 75 cents, it was supposed to be amazing.

"Then you put the chain on me, remember?" She laughed and it was a pretty, almost musical laugh. "You pulled the links tight and snapped the lock and then you said, 'Go ahead, Mrs. Claflin, see if you can get free,' but then your mother got upset with you and made you unlock me. Remember that?"

I did and was embarrassed.

"Do you still have that trick, Charles? I'd like to see you do it again sometime. It must be wonderful to have such a gift. Of course, I know it isn't magic, not really. I know there's always a way you could let me go free."

I wanted to tell her how it was done, maybe even show her again, because I enjoyed that trick. About the only person I ever showed it to who wasn't amazed was Mr. LeBlanc. He was sitting on the ground eating his lunch one day when I put the chain around his wrists and locked it. He just laughed and twisted his arms until the links of the chain spread open and handed it back to me saying he was sorry but he wasn't finished eating his johnny cake. It hurt my feelings at first and made me feel foolish, but Mr. LeBlanc fixed the chain after that and I realized there were some people who didn't put much store in magic.

"What *are* you thinking, Charles?" Pearl Claflin brought me back to the shady porch, to July, to the heat. She was picking up her knitting and a newspaper from the floor. She bent over with an effort, taking a deep breath and pushing her hair back as she stood straight again. The movements of her body were visible through the flowered dress, not just the plump curves, but slow, floating movements, soft shiftings of unseen flesh from one location to another. She never looked like that in her nurse's uniform.

148

"I say," she said, "what *are* you thinking of?" She smiled beautifully at me and I guess she knew I was looking at her.

"What I really called you for is a favor, Charles," she said, changing the subject and putting down her glass next to mine on the table. "There isn't a window in this blessed house of Navotny's that will open or shut right once summer comes. They all stick like they was nailed. Of course, my good-for-nothing Norman, bless him, says it's just the humidity and there's nothing can be done about it."

I drained the last of my lemonade. The ice cubes slid down and bumped my upper lip.

"You can have another one of those if you like, but you'll have to help me first!" She laughed beautifully again. "Come along . . ."

She led me into the house, through the sitting room then to the rear. I could see the kitchen straight ahead, but Pearl opened another door and marched into a dim room where the blinds were closed. There was a closet with white dresses hanging in it, chests of drawers, a long mirror on the wall, a big bed. I waited in the doorway.

"Come in, Charles, for land's sakes," she said, "it's just a bedroom." She pulled up a venetian blind, letting light into the room. I saw women's stockings on a chair. I looked away from everything. "This one's stuck tight," she said, "but I'm sure you're strong enough to open it for me. It's just not healthy to sleep without fresh air in a bedroom, you know."

I could feel the sweat on the palms of my hands. The house was quiet as a library. Pearl Claflin and I seemed to be the only people in all of Hancock at that moment. The bedroom was filled with a sweet scent, nothing like my mother's room which always smelled of the bug spray she used to kill elm beetles.

I pushed up on the window frame with the heels of my hands. It was stronger than I was. Pearl stood next to me, holding the curtains out of the way. The sweet scent came from her body in warm waves. I bent my knees, straightened my arms and pushed with my legs. The window lurched up an inch, stuck again, then slid free. There were deep red creases across my palms.

"Oh, wonderful," Pearl said. "That's just grand!"

As I wiped my hands on the seat of my pants, the hot, pungent scent of pines growing in the sandy soil around the house moved in through the open window. It made me want to be outdoors again.

"Now, how about another lemonade?"

"No thanks, Mrs. Claflin."

"You can stay a bit, can't you? I hate to see you work so hard for me and then just run off."

I wished she would turn and lead the way out of the bedroom, but she stood, unmoving, between me and the door. I wiped my hands again.

"I better be going," I said.

"I hope you'll stop by again when you have more time. Bring that chain trick too. I'd like to see that again."

My brain had held its breath so long that it must have blacked out, because I don't remember leaving the house and I forgot all about going back to Winter's attic. I just walked home in confusion.

26

AS soon as I was alone, I took my father's pistol out of the Louis Sherry candy box and held it carefully so it pointed at the garage floor. Mother had let me hold the gun once or twice in the past when I asked, but only for quick moments. Now I felt the gun was really mine, as if Father had given it to me, not just to hold but to keep. It felt much heavier than I remembered and seemed almost too big for my hand. The metal was mottled blue. The cold of winter seemed to be in it still.

I raised the gun, leveled the barrel at a window and looked down the sights at a spruce tree beyond. I wanted to pull the trigger, just to feel it move and hear the click, but I didn't dare for fear the gun might be loaded. I still hadn't figured out how it worked or how to open it to see if there were bullets inside. If it happened to have a bullet in it, and if it happened to go off, what better way to announce to the Territory that I had just taken Father's pistol from the top shelf of Mother's closet?

I had finally decided that if I was going to carry all that cash, I should be armed. As soon as I had Winter's money, I was going to need protection. Wherever I went after I ran

151

away, I was sure I'd be safer if I had a gun. And especially if I was going to run away alone, which was the way things looked now.

The next thing I would have to get was bullets. The pistol was a .32 automatic, made in Belgium, with the name Royal on the grips. I didn't know if all I'd have to do was ask for .32 caliber bullets or whether I would have to bring the gun to the store to get the right ones. And what store would I go to? I wished Mother hadn't been so stupid about throwing away Father's ammunition. I knew George didn't have any. I wouldn't want him to know I had Father's gun anyway.

I put the pistol back in the box and hid it in the garage.

I could feel my chest getting tighter as I started down the road. This, I had decided, was the day to get the money from Winter's attic before something happened to it. I hoped I wouldn't meet anyone and thought about cutting through the woods behind the Claflin house just in case Pearl might be knitting on her front porch again. But now that I'd made up my mind about the money, I was in too much of a hurry to go out of my way, so I walked right down the road, looking straight ahead. No one called my name.

The Winter house appeared as though it had been deserted for years. Grass was knee high and the old lilac bushes had grown thick and green in front of the downstairs windows. I cut across the fields, then along the edge of the gravel pit and around back to the cellar door. Everything looked the same. Fresh green creepers had started to grow over the old doorframe, which seemed to be a sign that no one had been inside. I yanked off the vines, pulled the door open and stepped down into the dank cool of the cellar. In a moment my eyes were accustomed to the dark and I saw that all the junk was still there. What a place for a fire!

I went upstairs to the kitchen, then to the second floor hall, finally up the steep flight that led to the attic. The house was hot as an oven and smelled of dry shingles.

At the top of the attic stairs, I stopped to listen. I heard a squirrel on the roof, nothing else. A filtered, milky light came through the fly-specked attic windows. I could see the dusty pile of old briefcases in the corner, just where they had been. I tumbled the top ones aside until I saw the small black box. It was all exactly as I remembered. I picked it up, went over to one of the windows for better light and sat down on the floor. Barnflies, wasps and elm beetles buzzed and collided against the glass. Spiders froze. I opened the case.

The money didn't look the way I remembered it. There were the same bundles of bills on top with withered rubber bands, but underneath, where I thought I had seen more money, I found only some timetables and train checks. I picked up the old bills and made one stack of them, then dumped the rest of the stuff onto the floor. There was no more money.

For a moment I wondered whether someone had come to the attic and taken most of that huge fortune I had seen weeks earlier, but then I knew that couldn't be. Why would anyone take only *some* of the money? I counted the bills with a feeling of disappointment and anger. Tens, fives, ones were what I had seen before, but there were now more ones than tens, it seemed. I arranged them all in $10 piles on the floor. Ten, twenty, thirty, forty, fifty . . . it was still more cash than I had ever held in my hands before, but it wasn't thousands of dollars. I looked at the stacks of bills—three piles of ones, two fives and ten tens. I had $140.

The Airflow was out, but $140 was still enough to buy a ticket to somewhere.

I put all of Winter's old railroad stuff, including his ticket punch, back into the case and closed the lid. I then made a roll of the money and stuffed this into my pants pocket. Now that it was only $140, I didn't feel as guilty about taking it. Anyway, I thought, it wasn't really Winter's money I was taking. He had stolen it from other people first.

I decided to go home through the woods instead of walking up the road with the money in my pocket. It seemed as if an amount as large as $140 would be visible right through my pants if anyone met me. I set off on a roundabout route that went through some of the places where Mother and I went every winter to gather greens for the Christmas wreaths. Well back of the Winter house was a path that would eventually lead me to the road near the Claflin's.

I didn't often scout through here in summer, but I remembered the way. I usually made my first trip to this part of the Territory in September when Mother would ask if I was going to make wreaths this year and was there a good crop of greens in the woods? Of course I always said yes, I was going to make the wreaths as usual, because I knew that's what she wanted. Besides, making and selling the Christmas wreaths wasn't really something I did alone. Like the root beer, Mother and I did it together. The wreath money went into the family fund.

By October I usually knew where all the best greens were growing. We didn't make our wreaths from coarse pine or cedar, we used only two small ground plants that were known in the Territory as "runner" and "bear grass" or "princess pine." Both species grew in the very shadiest areas of the woods where they pushed their feathery green foliage up through the humus of the forest floor.

"Plenty of good runner down back of Winter's," I would

say after an early-season reconnaissance, and even if it were still a warm fall day, Mother would seem to be serious in sharing my excitement at the discovery. Christmas was coming!

"Don't forget, you'll need more of that heavy wire for the rings this year," she would say. Or she'd remind me that we should have extra pine cones for people who ordered wreaths with decorations. The real truth was, I could not have run "my" Christmas wreath business without her. Sometimes, together, we made as much as $30.

I moved through those same woods now with almost five times that much in my pocket, more than we'd made in all our years in the wreath business.

This year's new crop of young greens was coming up strong and fresh. It looked like a good year for princess pine —but would I be picking any?

Even though it was August-hot in the woods, memories of Christmas came back clearly . . .

By November the big old burlap gunnysacks were usually down from the attic (Mother would mend last year's rips) and then when December arrived, maybe even earlier, we'd get out the list of last year's customers and start calling for orders. That was the most exciting part.

"I'll be making the wreaths again this year, Mrs. Howard," I'd say on the telephone. "You had a ten-inch princess pine last year. Would you like the same again?"

"How much are they this year, Charles?"

"Fifty cents for the ten-inch size. That's without decorations."

Sometimes Mother and I would sit at the kitchen table and try to think of new people Uptown who might be good prospects. She didn't like me to solicit "outright strangers," however. She considered it somehow indelicate if I was too aggressive about getting orders, especially from certain people.

"How about Mr. Fales?" I asked once. He was the richest man in town and Mother seemed to hesitate at first. Then she agreed.

"I don't see why not. He was a friend of your father's."

It was important to pick the green before snow fell in the woods, otherwise you simply couldn't find the small plants. Sometimes I would go harvesting alone early in December; later Mother and I would go together, walking down the road with the empty gunnysacks folded over our arms, turning off the road into a cart path, then finally to the area where the crop was healthy and plentiful. The two varieties were often found growing together, a soft green carpet under the tall trees.

"You certainly know your way in here," Mother would remark. "Where are we now?"

"Just back of Mr. Winter's place."

It was quiet work, gathering the greens. The soundless woods were disturbed only by the winter wind breathing in the tops of the trees and the hollow, ripping noise we made when pulling the small plants from the frozen duff of the forest floor. We didn't talk much as we picked, we just moved along, all stooped over, searching through the undergrowth in whatever direction the greens led. Gradually, the old patched gunnysacks would fill and then, when there was no longer enough light to tell healthy greens from yellowed ones, the two of us would straighten our backs with happy groans and tie the tops of the bags tight and trudge home in the dusk. Sometimes quail would frighten our hearts to lumps as a covey suddenly burst from the wagon path. Sometimes an owl spoke.

The woods didn't look the same in summer, but I found
my way to the path easy enough and followed it to where it
passed behind the Claflin house, unpainted and looking
pretty shabby from the rear. There was an empty tarpaper
doghouse in the yard with a rusty chain tossed across its roof.
I remembered when the Claflins had Queenie, the collie that
died. There were also oil drums, cement blocks left from the
foundation, a wheelbarrow without a wheel, a clothesline.
Two pairs of Mr. Claflin's Chinese pajama-pants hung side
by side, like a double suicide. Also some shirts, socks, a set
of window curtains, and on the end nearest the house, a
whole row of Pearl's long white nurse's stockings.

When I returned home, I put $130 into the Louis Sherry
box with Father's gun and rolled up two five dollar bills and
placed them into the nickle-plated, waterproof match case I
kept in my desk drawer.

27

A DUSTY ROAD was the single most delicious concoction that could conceivably be eaten anywhere, any time. A Dusty Road was a slithering, syrupy mound of pure pleasure that, when generously made, spilled over the edges and down the pedestal of the silver drugstore dish like a golden glacier and could take as long as ten or fifteen lingering, spoon-licking minutes to eat.

Unfortunately, because of its size and exotic content, a Dusty Road cost 25 cents in 1936. As a consequence, I knew exactly what one looked like, but couldn't be sure of the taste. In fact, I had never actually eaten one.

"Two Dusty Roads," I said to Mr. Walsh when he came to the booth to take our orders. Mr. Walsh ran the Rexall store that was the principal hangout of Academy students on Main Street. He was the pharmacist and he was also the man behind the soda fountain who made the Dusty Roads. He was famous for his creation.

"What's in a Dusty Road?" Annie Wendell asked.

"You shall see!" I had the two five dollar bills in my pocket.

"Have you had one before?"

"Lots. All us Academy kids have 'em here. He makes the best in town."

It had taken a burst of courage that I couldn't explain. I had spotted Annie Wendell when no town toys happened to be hanging around her and, in a wild blushing moment, I had asked her if she'd like a soda at Walsh's.

"You surprised me," she said. "You never asked before."

I had surprised myself. I think it was the $10 that was responsible. If I'd had $10 in my pocket that last time when Annie and I were fooling around in the old house, I might have kissed her right and not made a fool of myself.

"It's been a busy summer," I said, trying to sound like someone who had a comfortable allowance and came from Rye, New York.

Mr. Walsh brought the two dishes with spoons and paper napkins, and he put everything down on the table between us. The drugstore had only one small booth. During the school year, the booth was always taken by a certain group of boarding students, the same ones every afternoon. Reservations were no problem in August, however.

"It's beautiful!" said Annie. "What's it made of?"

I started with what I knew was on top, a heaping spoonful of powdered malt that clung to a runny layer of caramel encrusted with ground nuts. The base was a mountain of vanilla ice cream. I smoothed out the malt with my spoon.

Our spoons clicked on the metal dishes and our mouths were happily glued shut for a time. Mr. Walsh came to the booth before we were even half finished and said, "That'll be fifty cents." He was a man taught by long experience to get his money promptly from students.

I took one of Conductor Winter's fives out of my pocket and put it on the table.

"You rob a bank?" Annie looked at the money and then at me.

"I always have money," I said as casually as I could.

"I guess I should say I'm sorry," Annie said after a while.

"Nothing to be sorry about," I said, not knowing for sure what she meant.

"I was mean to you that day . . . remember? In the old house?"

"I guess I asked for it," I said nobly.

"That was just it. You didn't ask for it."

"I don't get you."

"I mean, most of the boys in this town always want something. They think they're smart and they think girls are stupid."

"It's okay," I said. "No hard feelings."

"I know, but I wasn't very nice. Can't I say I'm sorry?"

We both laughed a little uncertainly, but we laughed together.

"Pals?" I said, holding out my hand across the empty Dusty Road dishes. She looked surprised, but she took my hand.

"Okay. Pals," she said. Then there was a long pause while I tried to think of something to say to a new pal. There wasn't much concerning my life I wanted to discuss or that didn't embarrass me. Everything about me was so ordinary in some ways and so strange in others.

Finally I said, "I may be going away soon."

"More travels with your mother?"

"No, just by myself. I got things to do."

It didn't seem she believed me. She certainly didn't act as impressed as I thought she would be. She just smiled politely and waited for me to explain.

160

"I'm thinking of leaving town."

The words came out because I had no others ready. I couldn't stand awkward silence and I couldn't think of anything else; all that left was the truth. So the one thing I was never going to tell anybody, ever, had spilled out in the public booth at Walsh's Rexall drugstore in front of a girl I hardly knew and who I once thought loathed me.

"Leaving by yourself?"

I nodded. I had to finish what I had started somehow.

"You mean before school starts?"

"I hope so."

What was I telling her all this for? I couldn't believe myself. I was about to give everything away—the train ride, the visit to Gasoline Alley at Indianapolis, Fenway Park, Jean Harlow. . . . I couldn't explain all that, never in a thousand Dusty Roads. Why had I opened my big mouth in the first place?

"You mean you're going to run away?"

Now the very *words* were on the table, right out there between the empty dishes. The secret password of the whole summer, the sum total of all the lists, all the plans.

"I hate Hancock," I said, without looking up. I heard her start to say something in reply, but I wasn't listening. I was still hearing myself.

"I know," she said. "I hate Hancock too."

I pulled my attention back and looked at her. She was smiling. The cavity between her front teeth had been fixed.

"I've always wanted to run away too," she said evenly, as if there was nothing unusual about such an idea. "I've thought about it for a long time. But I wouldn't know where to go or how. I don't know anybody anywhere else."

Then it wasn't true that she had run away once to have a

baby. "You've never been away on your own?" I asked.

"You've heard that old rumor story too, haven't you?" she said, looking straight at me.

"What story?"

"About me having a baby. It's not true, never was. Some smart kid in Hancock High started it."

I laughed weakly and wanted to change the subject. But I was glad to hear the story wasn't true. Neither of us said anything for a moment, then she went back to our conversation, right where we had left off.

"How can you run away if you don't have a place to go?"

"Oh, I got places," I said, thinking of all the overnight cabins and motor courts I imagined along the highways out west. But I knew she was right. My $139.50 was going to go pretty fast if I stayed in expensive places every night.

"I'd do it if one of my brothers would come with me," Annie explained. "But they won't, and Ma and Pa aren't ever going to leave here either. It just can't ever work for a girl . . . but I wish it could."

Mr. Walsh came to the booth again and picked up our dishes. I didn't want to leave yet.

"You want some water?" I asked, hoping she'd stay a little longer and talk with me some more about this problem—our problem.

"Sure," she said. "The Dusty Road was terrific."

I asked Mr. Walsh for some water and he made a tired face. We sipped the water when it came, but somehow the time for confidences seemed to be over.

"I sure hope you don't go," I said.

"I hope you *do*!"

"I probably will. Before next month."

"Good. I understand, really. This is an awful place."

"You won't tell anybody what I said?"

"Who would I tell?"

I shrugged.

"Nobody really cares what we do anyway," she said. "It's our life."

Annie got up to leave and I slid out of my booth seat sideways. "Thanks," she said with her new pretty smile. "Let's stay pals, okay? As long as we're both around, that is."

We shook hands again.

It had been the greatest half hour of the whole summer.

I KNEW something must be wrong when I heard Ada calling me from Across-the-street. Ada never called. She knew what a fuss Mother made when I visited, so she used one of our agreed-upon signals any time she wanted me to come over—front parlor curtains pulled open or the porch light on or, in bad weather, she'd put the old covered roasting pan out on the front steps. (It usually contained a slice of pie.) I never failed to notice any of these secret signs, so there was no need for Ada to call, but on this August evening after supper, she was yelling my name with what seemed like fear and anger at the same time. Her voice sounded as though it came through a megaphone.

"I'm coming!" I yelled, whether she could hear me or not, and started to run. It didn't matter if Mother saw or heard because something very bad must have happened.

"Help me find George," Ada said as soon as she saw me. "He's gone."

I knew that *gone* must mean *gone,* not just gone-to-the-barn or gone-to-have-a-drink-in-back-of-the-hen-coop or gone-fishing-at-the-pond. Ada always knew when George was at one of those places and it didn't bother her, not like this. This must be different.

"He's got the rifle and I think he's got a bottle too," she said, shaking her old head in a mixture of sadness and despair. "We'd best bring the light," she added as we went into the house together. "It'll soon be dark in the woods . . ."

"The light" was the longest flashlight I had ever seen. George kept it in his den. It held six batteries in its black handle and had a large, nickle-plated reflector on the end. I knew where to find it.

"He's crazed with the drink," Ada said. She was sitting in her rocker, pulling a pair of black rubber galoshes over her felt slippers. "I don't know where he gets money to buy the stuff, he must be lying to me about what he needs for gasoline." I could see tears shining in the old lady's eyes now. I didn't understand how she could still feel motherly toward such an old man. Usually she only spoke of George as a "dam-fool" who would never change, but that evening I saw something else.

"Why would he take the gun?" I asked, looking at the empty place in the umbrella stand where my octagon-barrel favorite usually rested.

"I saw him sneaking it out to the barn this morning," she said. "I thought he was after a woodchuck . . . but it's not in the barn now."

"Would he take a rifle into the woods?"

"He would if he got a notion to scare folks off."

We went out the back door and down the path between the barn and the hen coop with Ada leading the way. She carried a long stick in her right hand and poked it into the ground for support as she walked. She wore an apron over her housedress which came almost to the tops of her galoshes. She would have been a funny sight if I didn't love her.

I was taller than Ada and could move faster in the woods, but I let her go ahead. It was her search more than mine. She kept talking without turning her head.

"If he's fallen somewhere, we'll have to look sharp . . ."

"When did you last see him?"

"Must be four hours."

The path was downhill. We went by the place where the old broken plow was all overgrown and rusting by the wall. If we turned right there, we'd get into the wild raspberry canes.

"He wouldn't have gone that way," I said.

"Crazy with drink!" Ada said, not listening to me. She was talking to herself. Her right arm went up and down with the stick like a steam locomotive with one piston. "When he's crazed, he might go anywhere!"

I was surprised at the old woman's strength. She was over eighty but she pushed her way through brush and young evergreens like a man. I was sure she would tire soon though, because between where we were and Airplane Pond the ground turned rough and the way was hard to follow. Mother, who must be thirty years younger than Ada, would never dare try to find her way in these woods.

"Hark!" said Ada, stopping. She held her stick straight in the air for silence. I heard nothing. "He's in here some-where," she said, lowering the stick slowly and suspiciously.

"Shouldn't we holler?"

"He wouldn't answer. Not when he's crazed, he wouldn't."

"Crazed" or not, I wanted to call out my friend's name. Maybe he'd been the lifetime despair of his mother, as she said, but he'd never hurt me. I wanted him to know I was looking for him.

Ada led on. "Sometimes he sets near here," she said, pointing with the stick at a dim clearing under big pines. Kids from Lincoln Street had nailed pieces of wood to the trunk of a large tree to make a ladder. I couldn't see how far up it went, but I knew it ended in a sort of platform that served as a treehouse.

"I found him at the base of that tree once, asleep," Ada said. "Wonder the dam-fool didn't try to climb it."

It was dark enough now to turn on the flashlight and its beam jiggled wildly as I hurried along. We were out of the old woods now, into a place that had been lumbered a few years before. The ground was a jumble of stumps, snags and slash with young trees coming up amongst the debris. They all stood about as high as a man and any one of them could have been George. But then, I thought, he probably wouldn't be standing. I put the flashlight beam on shape after shape. In the light, they all became trees.

"Hark!" said Ada once more, again raising her stick.

"George!" I called. "It's me!"

I thought I heard him cough.

"It's me and your ma!"

"He could start a fire easy enough in here the way he smokes."

She was right. I could picture the little pieces of cigarette paper that sometimes fell, still glowing, from George's home-made Buglers. But there was no smell of smoke, only the resinous perfume of the tinder, like the inside of a cedar closet in summer.

Ada halted, leaning on her stick. "I'm tuckered," she said, her wrinkled old face looking fierce in the reflection of the light. "I'll wait here," she said, "and you go on . . . go as far as you can and take the light. I'll be all right, I'll just set."

I didn't like leaving her in the dark.

"Go *on!*" she said. "Try the pond."

I had to get my bearings if I was to strike Airplane Pond. We'd wandered off the usual trail. I turned myself a little south of east and it felt right. "I won't take long," I told Ada.

"Take your time, boy. I'll just set here on one of these stumps."

"You sure you're all right?"

"Bah!" She waved the stick at me menacingly. "Look sharp!" she said. "He's here . . ."

I moved more swiftly now that I was alone, crashing through the dry stuff as loudly as I could so Ada would hear me go—and so George would hear me coming. They were both depending on me, I thought, my best friends. I felt responsible and older.

"George!" I called. "C'mon home!"

There was no answer. My light swept silently around in the wilderness but discovered nothing. The route brought me to the back side of Airplane Pond where there was no slope down to the water, just a tangle of brush. The permanent light of the summer sky came through the path in the trees and I could see the water. It wasn't flat, but seemed to tilt like a tin pie plate toward the side where George and I used to fish. Bug sounds were busier now than they had been in the pines. Nothing dimpled the water's surface.

I moved around the circle of the pond. Something caught my eye in one of the broken trees, something that was swinging like a rope, long and dark. I reached out and it felt like rubber. A piece of the plane, a piece that still hadn't made it all the way to earth.

I wondered what George had done with his scalp. Put it away somewhere, no doubt. Hid it with a bottle of Seagram's Five Crown. I stared a moment at the pond. Somewhere down there was a fallen war machine, with a lot of stuff in it still intact. I'd always been curious whether the instruments told a story. What was the pilot's airspeed? Did the

bank-and-turn indicator show a wild angle? Had his altime-
ter been correct?

I was coming around to the fishing place now and the sky
light turned to shadow. Also, the mighty six-cell flashlight
was losing some of its power, making only a yellow glow.

The first gunshot almost killed me, at least it seemed that
close. It came from straight ahead and I was sure it had
traveled right up the flashlight beam and through my body.
No make-believe shot-in-the-back that! For it pulled a hissing tail behind it.

"George?" I switched off the light. There was no sound,
but he must be within 50 feet. I crouched down, leaving the
light off. Why would he shoot at me? He knew my voice as
well as his mother's. Was he *so* drunk?

A bullfrog began pumping out deep, groaning notes at the
water's edge. That frog doesn't care if I'm scared, I thought.
But Ada must have heard the shot. What would she think?
Would she try to find me in the dark? How long had we been
in the woods, anyway? Was Mother ringing the sleigh bell
right now?

There was another noise straight ahead. A scratching
sound, like a wooden matchbox being opened and closed.
Then the unmistakable click of metal. The rifle bolt. Forward
and down. Locked.

The second shot zurped the surface of the water to my left,
rippled the whole pond and screamed off into the brush on
the other side. So, whoever it was wasn't actually shooting
at me, he was just shooting. But who had George's gun, if
not George?

The bullfrog fell silent now. Maybe he cared after all.
Maybe he was scared too.

"Who's there?" The question sounded silly in the darkness, especially after two rifle shots. My voice had quivered when I said it. "Who's there?" I asked again. Better this time. Stronger. "Aw, come on! Answer me! I'm trying to find George. George is missing!"

No one responded to my plea. My legs were getting cramped so I didn't dare put on the flashlight. I duckwalked about three or four yards, then I heard the scratching noise again. Click. Bolt. Lock.

The third shot might have gone straight up, I couldn't tell. It didn't ricochet or buzz off. Whoever was shooting didn't seem to know what he was doing. In other words, he could be drunk. And if he was drunk, then it was probably George.

"George?"

I could hear breathing, like George's dry leaves.

"Don't shoot any more, please! I'm right here. George?"

There was no answer and no more matchbox noises. I moved closer. The breathing seemed to quicken.

"I'm alone, George. Your ma's not with me."

I had my finger on the flashlight switch for what seemed ten minutes before I decided to risk another bullet by pressing down on it. Finally, when the bullfrog started up again, I thought it might as well be then. The button went down silently and I held it, moving the beam left and right in front of me. The light didn't penetrate the August darkness very well, but it fell on a huddle that was neither shrub nor tree nor pile of stones.

It was George.

He was where we always sat to fish, his back up against the big log, his head tilted over at a silly angle, his gray hair bristling. The rifle lay across his stretched out legs, pointing at the pond. When my light shone on him he moved, but in the yellow glow there seemed to be no expression or recognition on his face.

I stood up from my crouch and said, "Hi, George," trying to sound as if nothing strange was happening at all. I took a few steps toward him to see if he would leave the rifle in his lap. If he really was crazed, as Ada said, I must be careful. He might not recognize me in the dark.

"You all right, George?" I asked, coming closer.

His head moved awkwardly and his right hand fell away from the stock of the rifle. His left hand lay, palm up, on the ground next to him.

"You won't catch any fish here tonight, George," I said with a weak laugh and taking a few more steps toward him. "Unless you're planning on shooting a few," I added.

His eyes were on me, but his mouth was open. A thin trickle of saliva ran from the corner and fell on his shirt. When I saw this, I stepped ahead quickly and knelt beside him. His head tilted forward and flopped on my shoulder. He didn't say a word, but exhaled heavily and wearily. There was no smell of whiskey.

Whatever was wrong with George, I knew now he wasn't drunk. I also knew I couldn't just leave him there while I went for help. After holding him against my shoulder for a couple of minutes, I pulled away, got around behind him and tried to lift him upright. I had never realized before what a thin little man he was inside his old clothes. When I hauled him up and put my shoulder down under him, I was able to carry his whole body high on my back.

The rifle was another problem. I remember telling George that we'd have to leave the gun, but he didn't answer. He appeared barely conscious. I finally stopped talking to him because it didn't seem he could answer anyway, and off I stumbled through the dark woods, going by dead reckoning only, trying to find a path back to Maple Street. Sometimes I stopped to lean against a tree. While I rested I called "Ada!" into the trees several times, but there was no answer. I spoke to George again too, and told him everything was okay, we'd make it, we'd get out and he'd be fine. I didn't know whether he could hear me or understand, but just talking to him reassured me that he wasn't dead. His arms were flopping around like the meat that hung in Harry Byrd's butcher cart. I kept him on my shoulders because I was afraid that if I put him down, I might not be able to get him up again. My legs were beginning to ache and pains like needles stabbed near my kneecaps. But I knew I had to get George back to his house; he was part of my Territory, a piece of my life and all of a sudden I realized it.

My strength was just about gone when the big beam of light hit me full in the face and men's voices came at me from all directions. George's body was lifted off my back and I stumbled without the weight and sat weakly on the ground, feeling as though I might throw up. Someone put what looked like a policeman's jacket around me and helped me to stand again. I could see others carrying George up the path. Then, when the flashlight beams swung around, I recognized the back of George's barn. I'd been on the right course after all. I had almost made it home.

Ada was standing near the hen coop when we all arrived at the end of the path. She was still holding her stick. Mother was with her, her hands locked together the way she held them during thunderstorms. The two women didn't seem to be speaking to each other, but both made a fuss over me and Ada kissed and hugged me to the front of her apron without saying a word. She'd never done that before. Mother sniffed and put on a funny smile.

Annie Wendell was there with her big brother who was

drinking beer from a can. She smiled at me, but her brother just gave me a tough look that made me feel fourteen again.

It must have been past eleven before all the cars drove off and the neighbors went their ways and I finally got some answers to my questions about what really happened.

George had had a stroke. He hadn't been shooting at anybody, the rifle was the only way he had of telling us where he was. He loaded it one shot at a time with his right hand and then just pulled the trigger without aiming at anything in particular.

When they took him to the hospital he was alive and Doc Hersey said he might recover, but for the time being he couldn't use his left arm or left leg and couldn't speak. The doc said we'd all know better tomorrow how George was going to be. Meantime, he said, everybody ought to get some sleep.

Before I went to sleep, I started a list for the next day. Going back to Airplane Pond for the rifle was the only thing I could think of, however. Then I started to fall asleep. Police Sergeant Barrett's words echoed over and over: "He's a fine boy . . . no one could have done better . . . he saved the old guy's life . . ."

29

EVERY few days a letter about the Spanish shawl would arrive from one of Mother's friends. Some envelopes held checks or ten dollar bills and all had a note of some sort that she would read to herself. I was surprised. I didn't think anyone would fall for what I called the Shawl Scheme, but the lure of taking a chance, as Mother called it, must have been stronger than I guessed.

Mother put the money into a brown envelope with a string tied around the middle. She kept this in the living room closet, put away with all her bundles of stock-and-bond papers. By August, I was getting mighty curious to know how much had been collected and when the actual raffle was going to take place.

"We'll have a drawing soon," Mother said. "You can be the one to pick the winner."

"Have they all answered yet?"

"Not all, not yet," she said. "But they will."

I wondered how much money that would mean, but didn't ask. Mother's original mailing had been a big one, maybe a hundred names. If they all gave ten dollars, that figured out to a thousand dollars. Could the Spanish shawl possibly be worth that much?

One day, a chance-taker who sent ten dollars asked for a receipt. Mother became very indignant. "Imagine! Asking *me* for a receipt! What does she think I am, a thief?" Mother prickled over this for several days. She kept saying it was an insult for anyone to demand such a thing from an Investment Counselor and that she had a mind to send the ten dollars back with a note that she didn't want such a person to have the shawl.

Mother had a way of talking about people so you didn't actually know their name. Like President Roosevelt. He was always referred to as "that man in the White House"; it was the same with the Spanish shawl customers.

"Who asked for a receipt?" I said, thinking I would recognize the name if they lived Uptown.

"People like that needn't be discussed."

And that was the end of it. I don't know whether Mother sent a receipt after all, but I don't think she gave back the ten dollars. She just didn't say. The answer was somewhere in the brown envelope with the string tied around the middle.

"I think I'll give a cocktail party after the raffle," Mother announced grandly one day. When she said things like this, it always sounded as if she had just taken a part in a play and was rehearsing.

A party for all the winners and losers?"

"Oh, not for any of *them*!" she said. "For some of my good customers. It's been a long time since I've done any entertaining. We have the new landscaping this year—and summer parties are so nice."

I didn't understand exactly what Mother had in mind unless it was a repeat of her famous Planter's Punch Party a few years earlier when she invited some Uptown people for cocktails and then served only Planter's Punch and cookies.

I didn't really know anything about such parties when I was twelve, and I didn't even know what went into a Planter's Punch, but I was sure you were supposed to offer guests a choice of drinks and that ginger snaps didn't go with cocktails. But Mother didn't seem to care. She just kept telling everybody how much she loved Planter's Punch and didn't they too, explaining how she was "introduced" to the drink somewhere during her travels.

"Everybody drank them abroad," she said.

I noticed, however, that many of Mother's friends did not seem to favor the sticky, red concoction that Mother poured into tall glasses with mint leaves and powdered sugar on top.

I didn't wait to see how things would turn out that time. I was afraid it would all end up with the Souvenirs being displayed on the dining room table, so I skipped out and got lost in the Cedar Grove.

Was Mother thinking of doing it all again?

If so, I thought, I hope it will happen after I'm gone.

There were two weeks of August left when I decided to take a secret reconnaissance through LeBlanc's wagon path one afternoon and make some decisions once and for all. To make it more realistic, I brought the money and Father's pistol with me.

The route of the wheel tracks through the trees was a quiet one, as I walked until I reached the Hidden Command Post. From the looks of things, Mr. LeBlanc hadn't been through with Jimmy and Harry for a week or more. There were no fresh horse droppings, no wheel marks left by artillery caissons, no new lines of Signal Corps wire laid along the road, no indication that any big push against the Boche was imminent in this sector.

I accepted the salute of the sergeant on guard and made

myself comfortable in the C.P. I saw the field telephone, leather map cases, gas-attack alarm, sandbagged revetments and a single water-cooled machine gun emplaced nearby to protect the post. American soldiers had put up a rudely lettered sign: *They Shall Not Pass.*

I took the pistol from my pocket and laid it down. Then I counted all the money Intelligence had given me for the mission. There might be some dangerous moments, but a secret agent would know how to use cash when all else failed. One hundred and thirty-nine American dollars and fifty cents.

I remembered the last Dusty Road I had enjoyed as a civilian and the little ice cream parlor where I usually met Annie. How long before we would have another Dusty Road? I rubbed two quarters together in my hand and my thoughts wandered over miles to the beautiful girl I had left behind.

After a while, I ran out of imaginings. The soldiers disappeared. I looked up through the leaves at a summer sky in Massachusetts and thought about what might happen next. I didn't want to pick the winner of Mother's shawl raffle—it was silly and fake. And I certainly didn't want to be around if there was another Planter's Punch Party.

I held the pistol firmly in my right hand and aimed at a tall glass filled with red liquid and topped with green mint. This time, as I held the gun, I saw how the slide operated, how it opened the chamber and cocked the hammer at the same time. I pulled it back, let it spring forward and squeezed the trigger. There was only a dead click. Even if I could find the right ammunition, I thought, where could I shoot Father's gun anyway? I'd be caught.

And I'd probably get caught running away on the train;
I had to admit it. There were only two daily trains to Boston.
And when I got to Boston, where would I go after that?
There wouldn't be anybody at the Indianapolis Speedway in
August.

I couldn't quite understand how things had changed. In
April and May it had all been easy to imagine—thousands
of dollars, a new Airflow, meals in the dining car of the
Limited . . .

Summer had gone too fast. August was running downhill
toward the Academy.

I left the Command Post and headed home. I hid the
money in the garage again and, later, when Mother wasn't
looking, I put Father's gun back where it had been on the top
shelf of her closet.

"We're going to draw the winner on Sunday night,"
Mother announced at the end of the week. "We'll have a nice
supper in the living room the way we used to do and then
while we're having tea you can close your eyes and pick the
name! Won't that be fine?"

Sunday-Night-Supper-in-the-Living-Room was something I had loved as a kid. It was the best meal of the week
because it was not served in the kitchen, and instead had been
on the folding card table in the middle of the living room.
Mother would move the bridge lamp over for better light and
I'd get two chairs plus the lavender tablecloth with the tea
stains and embroidered flowers from the bottom drawer of
the sideboard and we would use the dishes with the black and
orange band around the edge.

The menu was always the same—toasted cheese sandwiches, grilled in butter in the frying pan until the cheese ran
out around the edges. Mother used her good teapot and

covered it with the quilted cozy and there would be Jell-O and cookies for dessert while we listened to the Sunday night radio shows. Jack Benny. Joe Penner. Ben Bernie. Charlie McCarthy. Major Bowes.

That was all right when I was ten and eleven and even twelve, I suppose, but it gave me a queer feeling now. I still loved grilled cheese sandwiches and could eat four of them at one time, but the idea of sitting alone with Mother, face to face across the card table, just the two of us holding a sort of tea party . . . I shuddered. What if Annie saw me doing that? Or even Artie? How could I explain I was doing it for Mother, because *she* still wanted to? Who would believe that *I* didn't like doing it too?

"I've put all the names on pieces of paper," Mother said, bringing a brown mixing bowl from the kitchen that held a few narrow slips of white paper jumbled in the bottom.

"How many are there?"

"There's as many as need be," Mother said with the smile that meant don't-question-your-mother. There didn't seem to be enough slips.

"Did we get a hundred?"

"Oh, lands sakes no, not a hundred. Close your eyes now," she said, clearing a space in the middle of the table for the bowl. She had made a regular party of it, everything the same as always.

"Are your eyes closed?"

"I'm ready." I wanted to ask what difference it made since I didn't know most of the people whose names were on the slips anyway.

"Go ahead then," she said, her voice rising gaily. "Pick the winner!"

I took the first piece of paper I could separate from the

others, opened my eyes and handed it to Mother.

Mother took the slip, held it under the edge of the lamp-shade, read the name and never changed her expression—which was serious.

"Funny that *she* should be the one," Mother said finally, almost as if talking to herself. She dropped the winning slip back into the bowl with the others.

"Who was it?"

"Someone who wouldn't deserve it," she said.

I didn't understand what Mother meant. The Shawl Raffle seemed to be going sour. "She wouldn't deserve it?" I repeated.

"I don't think that woman would know a genuine Spanish shawl from an afghan!" Mother was getting annoyed. Our Sunday night celebration was definitely over.

"Will she like it when she gets it, though?"

"Some people wouldn't appreciate anything, no matter what."

Mother started to clear the table, carrying dishes out to the kitchen and putting them into the white sink with a great clatter. She dumped the slips of paper from the bowl into the kitchen trash box behind the stove.

"Shall I go get the shawl now?" I asked.

"No need," Mother said. "Not just now."

"Are you going to write the lady? Or call her?"

"There'll be time enough for that."

Mother never notified the winner. I heard her telling people on the telephone that the shawl had been won by a dear and appreciative friend who lived in Virginia. But she never named her.

"How do the greens look in the woods this year, Charles?" Mother was asking her usual question, and right on time.

"Will it be a good year for the princess pine? That's the most important."

If I was slow to answer, the next question came quickly.

"We're going to make the wreaths again, aren't we, son?"

There was only one answer possible, even if I didn't know whether it was true or not.

"Oh, sure," I said. "We'll make the wreaths."

Actually, if I was still here when December came, I wouldn't mind. I sort of liked the whole business as a matter of fact. Just the same as root beer. Those were the times I liked my mother too.

The scene in the house when we returned from filling the old burlap bags with runner and bear grass was always a happy one, a prelude to Christmas reminding me of Dickens's *Christmas Carol.* The aroma of the greens filled the kitchen when the bags were brought in and dumped empty. It was a spiritous and cleansing smell, like a pleasant remedy for a head cold. Then, as heat from the stove penetrated the still-frosty bundles, it softened winter's grip on clumps of decaying leaves and pine needles, releasing an earthy musk like a premature spring.

"Never mind the mess," Mother would say. "There's no other way." And there wasn't. The kitchen table would be pushed to one side and chairs drawn up and boxes of tools and wire and string scuffed along the floor and the actual wreathmaking would begin, first with the cutting and shaping of wire hoops and then the gradual, cluster-by-cluster construction of the fresh green doughnuts, each handful of runner or bear grass being as artfully inserted on the circle as the flowers in a Union Street offering. We were proud of our three-dimensional wreaths, round and fully packed, not like the flat ones sold at the A&P. It was also a point of honor that our wreaths didn't need any shaping with shears to make them perfect.

Besides wire for the hoops, we needed other supplies and since Depression economics decreed that money never be spent when barter could be employed instead, we traded and salvaged. Soft copper wire, for example (very handy in the manufacturing process), came from a garageman who provided old automobile battery cables that I cut up and pulled apart. In return, he got a fifty cent wreath for free.

A number of customers ordered wreaths decorated with pine cones and other ornaments. These gilded touches were made possible when our helpful plumber came up with an annual supply of gold and silver radiator paint mixed especially for me in coffee cans. The cones were either the small, round variety from yellow pines or the long tapering ones from the Norway spruces near the barn. In winter these were usually closed tight as a fist, however, and had to be baked in the oven for hours before they opened. When fully cooked they looked like cinnamon-colored blossoms, crisp and warm, and filled the room with the scent of toasted pine pitch.

"It's too early to say about greens," I replied.
"Once school starts, you won't have much time for the woods."
"I'll go on weekends."

In other years, as Christmas drew near, the pace of wreath production usually picked up and after supper the kitchen became our workshop, the linoleum floor littered, rows of freshly gilded pine cones hanging from wires, the oven full of green ones snapping and clicking as they dried—and the back room, always cold in winter, beginning to overflow with finished wreaths.

182

After all the cash orders were filled, Mother and I made wreaths for our own doors, four of them, with the very best greens, prize stuff. The one for the front door was, according to custom, supposed to be our masterpiece. Of course, this was all in fun . . . or was it? We always went about making the last wreath almost reverently. Was there really some significance to the way this one turned out, an omen of some sort? I often wondered.

Anyway, the bear grass (never runner!) was chosen with the care used by a French chef selecting vegetables at market. Not too ripe, not too young. Beware of the type that yellows in the sun. The stems must be long, long enough to tie tightly and well. Everything was washed clean like preparing greens for a salad. Then bundle and tie, bundle and tie. It would take nearly two hours before the last green bouquet was in place and the season's masterpiece could be held up and admired.

"I think we've done it again," Mother would say.

Oh yes, one more ritual. During Christmas week, Mother always said it was time to take a ride Uptown and look at all the houses where our wreaths were displayed on front doors and windows. She didn't want anyone to catch her peeking, of course.

In earlier years this trip in the old Hudson was a Christmas tradition, a secret thing Mother and I did together.

Now, when I remembered, I had to admit that—especially at Christmas time—Mother wasn't so bad. She couldn't be Father, of course, but in her own way I guessed she loved me. And in my way, I suppose I loved her back.

At certain times.

GEORGE came home after two weeks in the hospital and Ada sat him down in his rocker in the living room, put a blanket over his lap and said that's where he would stay until he was better. It was near the end of August.

"He misses his toilet in the barn," she said, "but he'll just have to get used to the flush commode, like it or not. I certainly can't look after him if he's going out to the barn all the time!"

George could talk again, although he sometimes slurred his words and didn't swear as often as he used to. (He never did swear as much indoors as outdoors anyway, I noticed.) His left side was either paralyzed or so weak he didn't use it; I couldn't tell which, and I didn't want to ask. He needed help to walk and did everything with his right hand while his left lay motionless under the blanket. Ada said the doctors had told him he mustn't drink or smoke, not ever again, but she sighed and added she was sure he'd find a way eventually.

I thought he looked better than usual in some ways. He'd been given a proper haircut in the hospital which made quite an improvement and, despite the stroke, he seemed to have gained weight.

George didn't mention anything about the night I carried

him back from Airplane Pond and I couldn't tell whether he even remembered. I wanted to say something smart about what a lousy shot he was if he had been really trying to kill me that night, but I held my tongue. I didn't want to upset him with talk about an event he couldn't recall.

"How I hate to set, boy!" he said, smoothing the blanket in his lap. "Can't even see the garden from hare."

"Everything's growing fine, George," I said.

"Did that kohlrabi ever amount to anything?" It had been one of his vegetable experiments. Every spring, George selected an unusual seed variety from the seed catalog and planted it to see what would come up. In 1936 it was kohlrabi. It grew healthy as a weed, but after it was up, none of us knew which part you were supposed to eat, roots, tops or in between.

"Well, it's still alive—and uneaten," I said. The kohlrabi had been a joke all summer. We laughed about it together.

"Take anything you want from the garden," George said. "There must be tomatoes by now."

It was the cow that Across-the-street was most worried about. Somebody had to stake Buttercup out every day and milk her every night. At first, Ada had asked one of the Wendell boys to do this in return for all the milk he wanted.

"I don't want him doing it any more," said Ada. "He's never clean enough for milkin'. Those hands of his are right out of the tap and die shop! They're so grimy looking, I'm sure they'll taint the milk."

"Why don't you do it, boy?" said George, looking at me. "I showed you once."

He had, and I thought I still knew how to milk a cow. It was like driving a car. I'd seen it done enough so I was sure I could imitate the right movements.

"I'll try," I said.

"Come along then," said Ada, "you might as well start today." She picked up the milking pail from the pantry windowsill and led the way to the barn. "I'd do it myself," she said, "but I can't get up and down any more."

I slid the stool in close to Buttercup's flank, put the pail where Ada told me, then sat down and grasped the animal's soft, warm flesh. "Easy there!" Ada cautioned. "She don't know you that well yet."

After a few days, I had no problems with Buttercup—but I did with Mother, who couldn't understand why I had volunteered for such a job. "You're not a farm boy," she said. "Why don't they ask someone from around here?"

"I *am* from around here," I said. Actually, I surprised myself with that argument.

"But we're not farmers," Mother said with a sniff. "We're one of the oldest families in this town, we've been all over the world, and I don't want you in that barn every day milking an old cow!"

But that's where I went, happily. I was pleased with the responsibility I had been given and glad that I was able to do it right. Of course, I could have brought home all the milk I wanted but Mother would have none of that. Buttercup wasn't pasteurized.

I did other things Across-the-street. I fed the fish in the rain barrel more regularly than George ever did and I collected eggs for Ada and took care of the rabbits. One day, George asked me if I thought I could get the car started and then back it out of the garage. Naturally, I said yes. He handed me the keys.

It was the first time I had ever sat behind the wheel of George's Chevrolet, although I'd pretended many times that I was driving my mother's Hudson. I concentrated on the correct sequence that George had explained. First I pulled out the choke, then I turned the key, pumped the "acceluator" several times and stepped hard on the starter. After a few dry coughs that sounded like George himself, the old car sparked to life and sat vibrating on its springs. The smell of oil and gasoline fumes drifted up through the floorboards. Carefully, I put the shift lever in reverse, backed the car out of the garage, steered it in a half turn, stopped, pulled on the emergency brake and got out, leaving the door open and the engine running.

It was the first time I'd ever driven an automobile anywhere. My legs shook, my palms were wet. Even though it had only been for a hundred feet in the backyard, it was a *trip*—and a moment—I was sure I'd remember all my life. I stood looking at the old Chevy with new affection. It rattled all over and clouds of smoke came from its rear, but part of it was mine now and always would be.

"Let it run a while," George said from his chair when I reported the success of my maneuver. "Then put it away. And keep the keys with you if you want. I'd like you to start 'er up at least once a week, just to be sure she stays in running condition."

Keep the keys! If I want! It was like having my own car! Maybe next time—tomorrow?—I'd drive it all the way out to the end of the driveway, right to the edge of the road.

I decided not to tell Mother what I was doing.

August was the best time for blueberries in the Territory. There were plenty of the small, low-bush variety in the fields all summer, especially if there had been a grass fire a year or two earlier, but the biggest berries grew only on high bushes in certain places and that usually meant getting permission from the land owner.

Crazy Navotny had a fine stand of these bushes behind his house and at least once a summer Ada would call him on the telephone and ask if we could come down and pick what she called "a few pails." Navotny had no family and I don't think he ever picked berries himself, so the answer was always yes.

Because of George we were late going in 1936; but about the end of the month Ada sent me to see if there were any berries left on Navotny's bushes. When I came back and told her there seemed to be plenty, she said, "Fetch two pails from the barn and we'll go right now." This was good news because it meant pie.

Ada walked slower this year, but she still made steady progress. She just didn't lift her feet very high. If her gait looked awkward when we were walking on the pavement, it seemed better when we got into the woods. Resolutely, she led the way to the blueberry patch and started picking at once. It was just the way it had always been since I was nine or ten. The first handfuls of berries to hit the bottom of the empty tin pails sounded like ball bearings rolling around in a drum.

The cardinal rule of blueberry picking with Ada was never, never to eat a single berry, not one, until you got home. Naturally, this was hard for me to abide when I was a youngster, but there was no way to evade what was called Ada's Justice. This consisted of her looking inside my mouth, like a dentist, to detect any tell-tale blueberry stain on lips, teeth or tongue. If it was there, the verdict was swift and terrible: no pie for you, boy!

"I used to have the same trouble with George," she would say, tsking away as she picked. "Pick-two-eat-one, that was his way," she said. "After a whole afternoon, he'd have half a pail of berries and a stomach full of indigestion."

Now, I hoped, the time had come when I could be trusted.

The old no-eating rule had been intended to discipline only young children, I was sure. I took a chance that it wouldn't apply to a fourteen-year-old who could milk a cow, drive a car and carry people out of the woods on his back in emergencies. Every once in a while, I popped two or three good ones into my mouth (to test for sweetness and quality, I told myself), but if Ada noticed, she didn't say anything this year. The berries were warm and had so much flavor I was sure they would carry on my breath.

"Is George going to get better?" I asked as we reached and plucked, side by side. The berries made no sound now as they were dropped on top of others already in the pails. It was shady in the thicket.

"He's goin' to live, I'm afraid," said Ada. "But he'll never have full use."

"Good thing it's his left side."

"Don't matter. He won't drive a car again, no matter which side it is."

I wondered what would be the fate of the Chevrolet. Would they sell my car now?

"It could be worse," I said. "He'd be dead if he hadn't had the sense to fire the rifle that night."

"That reminds me," Ada said. "He's goin' to have a surprise for you. Don't tell."

"What is it? I won't tell."

"You recollect the rifle you fetched back from the pond?"

I said I did, of course.

"He knows how much you fancy that gun," she said, picking while she talked, "and since he probably won't ever shoot again either, he's aimin' to give it to you. But don't ever say I told you!"

The pails were getting full. There were many more berries in Ada's than in mine, as usual. I kept picking without saying more about the rifle, but my heart was beating fast. If it was a secret, I knew I shouldn't ask more. But eventually, curiosity was too strong.

"When is this going to happen?"

"Christmas, I 'spect. He says he's going to wrap it up and all. Don't you let on, now!"

"I won't," I said.

I counted on my fingers. September, October, November, December. Four months and the Octagon Barrel would be mine.

S EPTEMBER arrived, but summer stayed. Nothing changed, only the picture on the Currier and Ives calendar. Heat, thunder storms and cicada songs were the same; the scent of skunk in the evenings, the fragile tinkling of the Japanese wind chimes when a breeze stirred across the front porch, the creak of the wicker chairs, like thousands of tiny knuckles cracking when you sat down. Horsedrawn mowing machines tick-ticked as they sheared nearby meadows, milkweed pods ejected whole battalions of tiny white parachutists who floated off to fall on distant fields while the familiar voice of the play-by-play announcer came through screen doors everywhere.

The Red Sox were struggling to finish in the first division, George continued to sit in his chair, the Winter house remained empty and when I could see them, which was seldom, the two fish in the barrel didn't seem to have grown since spring. The ill-tempered rabbits still huddled, uneaten and unloved, in their cages, their white feet stained by their own olive-green droppings. The red ants never stopped their summer war games, the banty hens and roosters strutted around the driveway pecking dry sand, Buttercup grazed in circles of grass that had her tethering stake at the center and her chain for a radius.

No one in the Territory was really free to leave.

I drove the Chevrolet to the edge of the road almost every day, watching the gas gauge and worrying that when the tank was empty, Across-the-street wouldn't fill it again. Why should they? Gasoline cost twenty cents a gallon. What good was it for me to have $139.50, I wondered, if I couldn't use even a dollar of it to buy gas? The money was useless—until I ran away.

Time for that idea was ending too, however. When I went Uptown these days I saw cars gathering in the Academy drive. Teachers coming back early. I spotted the headmaster's Packard. On the athletic field, the goal posts had been given a fresh coat of white paint. The school's big power mowers rolled up and down the football yardlines and across the great front lawn, swinging smartly around the blue spruces, running true along the walks between the buildings. It wouldn't be long now. Soon everyone would be returning.

One day I heard the school's electric bells being tested, the angry rings that marked the beginning and end of classes. The sound drifted across the Academy lawn like an alarm announcing the end of summer. If I was going to do anything about escaping before that bell began to ring in earnest, my deadline was near.

I knew this for sure when Mother told me to get a haircut.

"We have to buy you some new pants for school," she said, "and I won't take you into Lewis' store looking like that."

Lewis' store never had anything I liked. Mr. Lewis always pulled up hard on the back of new pants when I tried them on and told Mother they fit fine and were just what all the Academy boys were wearing this year.

He never addressed any of his salesmanship to me.

When I went to John's barbershop, I took fifty cents of my money along with Mother's haircut allowance. I felt much older as I walked into the shop than when I had been there in May. John looked different too. The summer had sagged his face and made him look older. His breath still smelled like my idea of a Turkish kitchen.

"Hi, John!" I said, trying to sound casual and act like a regular and frequent customer. I had already made up my mind to have an egg *shumpoo* and then give John the rest of the fifty cents as a tip. It was a luxurious feeling.

"You grow, boy!" John bellowed, putting his paper down and slapping his big paw on my shoulder. "You grow!" A new picture of FDR clipped from the newspaper was stuck to the mirror in front of the dentist chair, but everything else was the same, including the empty Wildroot bottles. I sat and John covered me with the old striped apron and pumped the chair up with two strokes on the foot pedal. I felt his fingers measuring the long hair at the back of my neck.

"The usual, John," I said. "School starts next week."

I wasn't going to say anything about the *shumpoo* yet. John reached for the electric clippers. The apron was too tight around my neck. I could feel barbs of other's people's hair starting to prickle my skin. The clippers whined in my ear and smelled of sparks and old oil.

"You get a piece this summer, boy?" John was breathing through his mouth and pretending to whisper the question. I could feel cool air on the skin of my neck where the clippers were shearing off June, July and August. When I didn't answer, John came to his own conclusion.

"Ha! You got a piece, don't you? You got a piece at last, boy!"

I was amused. Flattered too. How could I tell him the truth? I didn't want to disappoint him. John seemed to live for the good news that some girl, somewhere, had given herself up to some deserving boy. There was no other way to explain it.

"No wonder you grow, boy! John told you, didn't I? I said, 'You get a piece, boy, you grow!' Now you see! You grow. You purify the blood."

What if he asked questions, I wondered? What would I say? He wouldn't expect me to say *who,* would he?

Who indeed, I wondered.

Hair fell like summer's grass in front of a mowing machine. Then the scissors snipped and clattered against the comb briefly, knocking on my newly exposed scalp. In minutes, my appearance was all changed. My summer hair had looked like Artie Wiggins'. Now I looked like . . . what? Rye, New York?

"You need *shumpoo,* boy."

"Okay, John," I said, watching his expression in the mirror.

"*Shumpoo?* Today?" I had surprised him. I smiled.

"Yeah, sure. Make it an egg *shumpoo.*"

"Egg?" John's face went blank.

"Yeah, John, egg. School starts next week."

He didn't have an egg so I said a regular *shumpoo* would be fine. He said he would go out and get an egg. I said never mind. It wasn't the egg, after all, it was the idea of the thing. John was disappointed. After years of trying to sell me an egg *shumpoo!* He sat me down on a straight chair in front of his small wash basin and told me to put my head down and close my eyes. Warm water ran over my head and down my neck and dribbled off my chin. I kept my eyes closed.

"You got *young* girl?"

It was easier now to lie because he couldn't see my face. "Not too young, John, just nice."

194

"I'm happy. You good boy." He was lathering the soap. It smelled like tar.

Actually, I thought, if we were going to talk about girls, I had my choice of summer adventures to remember. But I ought to have only one in mind. Should it be Annie, alone with me in the empty house? Annie giving me a chance that I muffed completely? Or nurse-mother Pearl? Pearly Pearl, all round and white.

I decided on Pearl. If I was going to make things up, it would be easier if I thought about her. Annie was almost my age, she was okay, she was real. But Pearl was made for lies. I thought John would like to hear about her anyway.

"You find a place to go with the girl? You got a car?"

"Nah, John, I won't be sixteen for another month," I lied.

"If you got no place, it's no good." The lather hissed in my ears.

"We had a place."

"Alone, that's what you got to have."

"Yeah, we were alone."

With my eyes closed, I let the afternoon with Pearl come back, the porch, the lemonade, going into the house, down the hall, into the bedroom. I pressed my head deeper into the basin. John's voice sounded farther away.

"You lucky . . ."

"Yeah." The word roared inside the bowl.

I saw Pearl standing in front of me in the bedroom with her uniform on, all white and clean and tight on her body. The room seemed like a hospital, white and cool, with a bed that adjusted up and down and a table that rolled on wheels and a folding screen in the corner of white cloth panels. There were some white flowers standing in a vase and a bright light overhead. I felt as if I had been brought in to be treated following a serious accident—an accident that, for some reason, caused me no pain, but was all the more critical because it didn't hurt. It was a *white* accident, not bloody like a cut or painful like sunburn, but more like being struck by a blinding flash of lightning. I required immediate attention.

John was soaping my head for the second time. I could hear the suds rinsing down into the basin. I kept my eyes closed.

"You get a good woman first time, that's important for young man."

"Yeah." The word echoed again.

Pearl had disappeared from the basin temporarily, but her voice was still there, clear and young, telling me I would be all right, just to keep my head down for a few more minutes. And by the way, did I bring the magic trick I had promised? "Your wonderful trick with the chain?"

Soon I could see her again. She was moving behind the folding screen, just her red-blonde hair moving back and forth behind the white panels.

"Hey! You like brunette?" John was laughing. "You like brunette?"

I didn't want my dream to end, so I didn't want to talk. It didn't seem necessary to say that Pearl wasn't a brunette. What did John care anyway? He was only talking.

I didn't hear Pearl return to the room because her bare feet made no sound on the smooth floor and there was no starched rustle from her uniform. She just slid from behind the screen and in the white glare of the room she too was white, white on white, milk in a white bowl, as marble-white and silently naked as a statue: powdered white, soft white, bread-dough white, warm white. Like a statue, she had no hair anywhere, but when she walked toward me, her breasts swayed. They were creamy white, but incomplete. They had no nipples.

196

"Rinse now!" said John as he dumped cold water over my head. It ran down my neck and over my eyes. I opened them one at a time to test for soap. All I could see was the inside of the basin. Pearl was gone.

John nudged me up straight and started rubbing my head with a towel. *Shumpoo* was over. John said he was sorry, it would have been better with an egg. He combed my hair straight back, examined my upper lip and said my beard would certainly grow heavy now that I'd had my first piece.

"Here," I said awkwardly, handing John three quarters and a nickel.

He looked at the coins in his hand. "Too much," he said.

"It's for you, John," I said. "Keep it."

He smiled. "You growin' fast," he said. "You're a man now, boy."

I thanked him. I was reassured. I hadn't told him the truth, but he still thought I had grown up. Someday, I wouldn't have to lie.

THE Hancock Hardware truck rattled into our driveway late Thursday morning with Mr. Palumbo at the wheel. His son Johnny was with him.

"Your lucky day, son," Mr. Palumbo said, going to the back of the truck and reaching for the chain that held the rear gate shut. Johnny went to the other side. When the tailgate of the truck dropped, two boards were run out to make a ramp and Johnny hopped up inside.

"Is your Ma home?" Mr. Palumbo asked. He was our family plumber, the one who gave me the Christmas paint, but the only time he ever came to the house was when pipes froze or a toilet wouldn't flush. I couldn't guess why he would be here today. A rumbling sound came from the back of the truck.

"She's inside," I said.

"I'll just tell her it's here."

It emerged from the truck into the glare of the noonday sun. Johnny Palumbo guided *it* carefully down the ramp to the ground. Silver paint and gilt were shining against black and red enamel, loops of chain growled softly against sprockets and sharpened steel sheared briefly against sharpened steel to make the sound that only a new lawnmower can make. A *power* lawnmower.

"You going to be the one to run it?" Johnny Palumbo asked. He was about seventeen and played football for Hancock High.

"Yes," I said, "I'll run it." I didn't know what I was saying at that moment, but I said what I hoped would be true. Run it! Would I ever run it! If this beautiful 21-inch Ideal Power Mower was by some marvelous quirk of fate going to be mine to run, I'd run it like the pace car at Indianapolis!

"It has gas in it already. You put it in here." Johnny laid his finger on a shining brass cap on a small, barrel-shaped fuel tank mounted on the engine top. The end of the tank carried the name: Ideal.

"You pull back on this starter crank . . . like that!" The engine coughed a cylinderful of blue smoke, caught, roared, then idled down as Johnny touched the throttle. The whole beautiful rig just sat there, vibrating slightly as the engine purred pure power. The front wheels were aimed straight down the side of the driveway toward the garage.

"Go ahead," said Johnny, "run it." He pointed to a handle that controlled the clutch. When I pushed in on it, the Ideal Power Mower jumped ahead, its chains all singing, its muffler popping, its gleaming array of blades hissing as they turned. The smell of green grass immediately mixed with the smell of exhaust. I was being taken to the garage! Behind me, a beautiful, 21-inch swath of smoothly mowed lawn lengthened like the wake behind a speedboat. Best of all, I wasn't pushing. In fact, I was pulling, trying to hold back against the inexorable strength of this marvelous machine, afraid it would just keep right on going, mowing through everything in its path.

I managed to stop the Ideal and get it turned around at the end of the driveway. Then I came back, trying hard to steer a straight line as Johnny Palumbo watched. Behind me, the mowed stretch increased to 42 inches! In only minutes, almost four feet of lawn had been cut and all I had to do was walk along and watch it happen!

Mother and Mr. Palumbo were standing at the end of the porch when I completed my round trip. Johnny reached down and shut off the engine so we could hear.

"Do you like it, Charles?" Mother asked, all smiles.

I said it was wonderful, or something like that. I didn't want to talk, I wanted to start the engine again.

"Well, it's all yours now," Mother said and I saw Mr. Palumbo nodding and taking backward steps and folding something into his shirt pocket. As he walked by me, he put his hand on my head. "Have a good time," he said.

"I thought it was the best thing I could do with that money from the Spanish shawl," Mother said after the Hancock Hardware truck was gone. She was still standing on the porch, enjoying the event. "They had it on sale for the end of the season."

I didn't wait for any more explanations of finance. I reached for the starter crank and pulled and the Ideal Power Mower answered its new master with a growl of power. Forty-two inches soon became eighty-four and seven feet became fourteen and I was half finished with the south lawn before I heard the sleigh bell calling me in to lunch.

"I thought you deserved it after the way you've worked all summer," Mother said at the table. "It was a hundred and twenty dollars, just the amount of the shawl money." She looked at me as if she wanted some response to this.

"I'd rather have it than the shawl," I said, meaning a joke, but ignoring that we now had both the Spanish shawl and the mower. I knew there was something wrong with this, but who was I to decide? Anyway, I didn't think having the mower was exactly Possession of Stolen Property. Mr.

Palumbo had been paid for it. It was mine. The shawl was Mother's problem.

I spent the rest of the day and almost all Friday mowing Versailles. I finished the South Lawn soon enough, then the circle around the Paddock, the Peony Path, the Avenue Français. I mowed in places where I had never been able to push the old hand mower and mowed some areas twice just to see how smooth I could make them. Through it all, the Ideal Power Mower never faltered, although the gleam of its new paint was soon covered with grass cuttings, seeds, dust and dirt.

Late Friday, before supper, I stopped cutting grass because there was no more to cut and cleaned the mower until it looked as bright and new as when it had come out of Mr. Palumbo's truck. Then, while Mother was busy in the kitchen, I wheeled my prize rapidly Across-the-street. The noise of the engine brought Ada to the window where she and George usually sat.

"What's that, for land's sakes?" she said, peering out through the screenwire, but knowing well enough what it was.

"It's mine," I said. "It's an Ideal!"

I heard George coughing as he tried to say, "Ideal! I'll say it's ideal!"

"Can you see it, George?" I couldn't see him through the screen.

"He can see it," said Ada.

"Your ma bought that?" George said. "Stocks must be up!" He laughed and coughed again.

"Watch," I said. "I'll show you . . ."

"Ain't nothin' new about it," Ada said. "It's just a lazy boy's lawnmower!" She laughed and waved her off-and-be-gone-with-you.

"I'll cut your front lawn if you like," I said without thinking of the possible consequences of such an impulsive offer. All I wanted was more grass to cut. I was in possession of infinite speed and power and a half a gallon of gasoline, the race wasn't over and the huge Indy crowd was still in their seats.

"You better ask your ma," Ada warned. But I didn't listen. In the next twenty minutes, I mowed Across-the-street's small patch of lawn and wheeled my great new machine smartly back to our side of Maple Street just as the sleigh bell was ringing for supper.

"Where were you cutting just now?" Mother asked. The question replaced my appetite with faint fear.

"Across-the-street."

"You were mowing *their* lawn? With *my* lawnmower?"

"Somebody's got to . . . neither of them can any more."

"I didn't buy that mower to have you go around cutting the neighbors' grass, Charles!" Mother was annoyed.

"Okay," I said.

"That mower cost a lot of money. It isn't to be used on others."

"Yes, Mother."

"They can get somebody else to mow their lawn."

I nodded. I knew Mother would forget about this after a while. By next summer she probably wouldn't even remember.

Then all at once I remembered.

Tomorrow was Saturday. It was the beginning of the last long weekend of Summer, 1936. Either I must run away right now or it was going to be another year at the Academy and in Hancock for me.

.... *33*

FALL scented the air. Elm leaves were turning yellow. Butternuts let go and dropped. It was the last Saturday of summer, my Last Chance. The thought frightened me, like the arrival of a final exam.

After breakfast, I brushed my teeth, put some long-lasting Brilliantine on my hair instead of water and walked as casually as I could through the kitchen. I didn't want to be noticed; I only inhaled. I'd let my breath go when I was outside the house.

Mother was ironing the pongee shirt again.

"Don't go too far," she said, seeing me heading for the door.

"I won't."

"Be home for lunch."

I wouldn't make any promises, not today.

"Er . . . I'm going to be at the Academy . . ." I didn't finish the lie.

"So soon? What do you have to do up there before school even starts?"

I said I wanted to see some kids . . . to get my locker key early . . . pick up a class schedule. Nothing sounded true.

"But you must eat lunch!" Mother insisted.

"I'll get something, don't worry," I said, sliding toward

the back door. As I was leaving, Mother issued some last instructions that I didn't hear and didn't care to understand.

The screen door slammed behind me before I remembered to count. (I never did make it to *five,* by the way, never reached the lilac hedge before getting shot in the back by that door.)

I went Across-the-street and took Buttercup from her stall, staked her out on the north side of the barn and said goodbye to her. I put my hand on her broad head, up between the horns. She tossed her muzzle and glared at me with one brown eye. What does a cow know anyway? George always said cows were the stupidest creatures of all and I guessed he was right. I knew it was silly to talk to a cow, but I told her what was on my mind anyway.

"It may not really be goodbye, old girl," I said. "But I want to try something for myself. I dunno how it's going to turn out." Buttercup went on chewing.

I thought about starting up George's Chevy, but decided there was no point in doing that one more time. I was tired of going nowhere in that car, anyway.

I returned to our side of the street, went to the garage and took $139 from its hiding place and pushed the roll into my pants pocket. I also took the Mt. Washington wallet with my father's last hunting license in it, the pocket compass, the pearl-handled penknife, a pack of Chesterfields, and the Blue Sunoco map of the *United States East of the Mississippi.*

One last look at the Hudson and then I scrambled across the south field to the shelter of the cedar grove. I went in one side and straight out the other, however. I didn't even check on the ants.

I crossed the next meadow at a run, slowing just as I hit Maple Street. I had reached a place on the road out of Mother's sight.

Uptown, the Academy yard was jammed with arriving cars and people. I saw students talking and waving, holding their portable phonographs and tennis racquets. The girls kissed, the boys punched each other on the shoulder muscles. (I never saw anyone else in Hancock do that, ever, but boarding students always seemed to be doing it.) I heard their laughter.

I kept on walking until I came to Depot Street and the railroad station. For some, it was a day of returning, I thought darkly. For others, it could be the day to get out.

I knew that only one train left Hancock on Saturdays, the 9:33 A.M. to Boston. However, the ticket office was always closed on weekends, so I would have to pay the conductor once aboard. There was a small irony in that, I thought. I'd be giving one conductor's stolen money to another. The railroad would be getting its cash back at last. What would old man Winter think of that, I wondered.

In the station, the clock over the ticket window showed 9:20. It moved in one-minute jumps, making a two-tone noise each time, *buzz-clunk.* It sounded loud in the empty waiting room. I was alone.

I decided to take my usual seat on the baggage cart outside. If the train was on time, I had 13 minutes. I leaned back against the peeling paint of the station wall and lighted a Chesterfield. It seemed long ago that cigarettes had made me choke or my eyes water. It also seemed a long time since that day I had seen the Great Train come through here. Could I make it reappear now, I wondered, the same steaming, impatient giant? And would the conductor and trainmen in blue serge and shining brass buttons climb down the steps and walk the length of the coaches with their gold watches held out stiffly at the end of gold chains?

For a moment I saw a man in a business suit appear at one

of the train's open doors. He looked up and down the tracks with annoyance. Seeing me sitting on the baggage cart, he called out.

"Where are we? What is this place?"

"Hancock, Massachusetts, sir."

"Where?"

"Hancock, sir."

"What's that near?"

But the man dissolved before I could tell him that Hancock wasn't near any place, not really. Hancock was Hancock. Then the train faded too. It was an effort for me to make the scene stay real, to keep it alive. But why try, I thought? There was no such train, I knew that. There never had been. I didn't mind admitting the truth to myself now. I didn't have any need for an imaginary train anymore, anyway. I was waiting for a real one.

The 9:33 arrived on time, its iron wheels sliding to a squealing stop. A young trainman stepped wearily down from an open door, looked up and down the station platform, saw me sitting on the baggage cart.

"Boward!" he called, still looking at me as if to say, "If you're taking this train, son, you better move quick!" Then he waved his arm in a stiff arc, the locomotive gasped and gave a lurch and the string of coaches rang together like iron bells as they began to roll slowly forward. The 9:33 was starting to move toward Boston.

I could have still run to catch it. I could have jumped down from the baggage cart and made it to the moving train in four or five good strides, easy. I could have grabbed the handrail and hopped onto the bottom step. I could have swung aboard almost as smartly as the trainman himself.

I could have, that is, if I'd really wanted to. And I guess

you could say that that was the exact moment my great plan to run away finally ended.

When the train was gone from sight, I walked up Depot Street to Main Street. Some of the early-arriving Academy boys were already hanging around Walsh's. I went in.

"Hey! There he is! How are ya, day hop?"

"Fine. Fine."

"You been here all summer? How's the Hancock Humper? You get much in this town?" They were in a jovial mood. One of them was the captain of the swimming team. He was a senior, blond and slope-shouldered and well-coordinated. All the girls were crazy about Pal Pennick.

I sat down at one end of the booth and told Mr. Walsh I wanted a Dusty Road.

"Coming up!" Mr. Walsh seemed in a good mood too. His big-spending boarding students were back after a long, dry summer.

"Lots of malt, please," I said.

"Lots-of-malt, right you are!" Usually Mr. Walsh said, "Everybody-gets-the-same-amount, who-do-you-think-you-are?" Or "Are-you-paying-extra?"

"Where'd you go this summer, day hop? What you do? You comin' back to school, aren't you?"

"Oh, I went to ball games and stuff and took the train to Maine. I know a girl up there. Went to see her."

"Yeah, yeah, that's the ticket." They were all drinking Cokes and talking about where they had been—Maryland, New Hampshire, Hawaii. There were girls in their stories too, and cars—and girls-in-cars.

"What was she like? The one in Maine . . . hey! C'mon, tell us!"

"Really nice. She was perfect, in fact. Her name was Roxanne. What a girl! She taught me plenty. She showed me things I never imagined a girl would know. We had the place all to ourselves. A whole house. We'd drink beer and just sit around doing nothing except when we wanted to."

"One Dusty Road!" Mr. Walsh put the dish down with a flourish and stood wiping his fingers on his apron, waiting for his money.

I pushed my hand into my pocket and felt the money. I knew there were some dollar bills on the outside of the roll, but my pocket was so tight I couldn't peel one off. I had to take the whole thing out.

"Will you lookit that! Geez! You sure didn't spend everything in Maine this summer, did you?"

Everybody's eyes were on the money. It looked like a bank robbery. I thought I had to explain.

"It's not mine," I said as casually as I could. "Just some of it . . . it's mostly a collection we took up for a friend. I'm going to give it to him soon."

"Too bad," the Academy boys said, some of them seeming disappointed, though really not caring. I gave Mr. Walsh a dollar. He went away with it. But he had also seen the rest of the money. Would he call the police?

"Hey, day hop's buyin'! Four more Dusty Roads!"

Mr. Walsh came back with three quarters in his hand.

"Four more?"

"Nah, we're kiddin', Mr. Walsh. Day hop's rich, that's all."

I started to eat, but the Dusty Road didn't taste as good as the one I had had with Annie.

"Hey, day hop, you do any swimming in Maine this summer?" Pal Pennick was asking me a question!

"Yeah, some, not much, a little . . ." (I wasn't a very good swimmer, or a very good liar.)

208

"You ought to go out for the team. We need a good man for the distances." Pennick seemed serious. He was swinging his arms around in exercise movements, stretching his muscles.

"I don't think I can."

"C'mon, why not?"

"Other reasons."

"Think about it. We could use you."

Pal Pennick wasn't such a bad type, I thought. He'd never talked to me before. But then, I never went to Walsh's.

"Gotta go," I said. The clock on the wall said eleven-thirty already. I hadn't finished the Dusty Road, but I felt restless. It had been a morning of big decisions. I was still thinking about them.

"See ya . . . see ya around."

"Yeah. See you Tuesday."

I was sure now that I had better get rid of the money. It just wasn't any use to me. I couldn't spend it 25 cents at a time all year. Eventually it was going to get me in trouble and I'd have to explain where it came from.

I was wondering what to do as I walked toward Maple Street.

John the barber was standing behind his big plate glass window as I passed. He waved at me with his rolled up newspaper and stepped to his open doorway. "My boy!" he roared good naturedly. I was afraid he was going to holler out, "You still getting your piece?" but he didn't.

"Hello, John. How's things?" I stopped.

"Same," he said. "Always the same in Hancock."

"No business?"

"The same. About the same." He slapped at a fly on the window with his newspaper.

Academy students never went to John's barbershop. He

was just a one-man shop and in the wrong part of town.

"If you had two chairs, would business be better, John?"

The old man's face lighted up like a jack-o'-lantern with bad teeth.

"Two chairs? John die happy!"

I knew then what to do with some of the money.

"Here, John," I said, stepping into the shop with him. "I took up a collection for you . . . it's fifty dollars for the other chair you want, the one at Bechtel's."

Of course, he didn't believe me. It was absurd. A kid turning up with fifty dollars.

"You steal?" His smile vanished.

"Nah, John, it's for you. Take it. What difference?"

"You steal from you Ma?"

"No. It's not stolen. I found it."

"What do you say? What's a collection?"

"That's just what I call it, John. It's like a raffle. You take a chance and maybe you win."

I peeled off five ten dollar bills without letting him see how much more money was in the roll. I pushed the cash into his hand. I felt him push back, his hand still closed against mine.

"I never take nothing that wasn't right," he said. "All my life, I just work, never steal."

"C'mon, take it. If you don't, I'm going to give it to someone else. And don't tell anybody." I kept my eyes on his face. I felt his hand open, felt the bills move from my fingers to his, like a note being passed in school. John's expression was a secret code.

"I do need another chair," he said in a new, calm tone of voice. "Now I think I'm going to get it this week."

34

L ABOR DAY was one holiday I never understood. Nobody worked, but nobody in Hancock celebrated anything, either. Why should a Monday that came at the end of summer and the beginning of school be a holiday? It didn't make sense.

Mother was taking up the cuffs on the pants she had bought at Lewis'. They were dark green and what she called worsted and they were going to be too hot to wear to school tomorrow, but there wasn't going to be anything I could do about it.

"You want to look nice, don't you?"

I went out. I wandered, first to the garage. I filled the gas tank on the Ideal Power Mower. Then I took what was left of the money from my cubbyhole and stuffed it back in my pocket again. I thought about things to buy. A new baseball. Mother would never notice that, maybe even two.

I went over to the cedar grove and watched the ants for a short time. I could buy them a whole pound of bacon now if I wanted. A whole pound!

I went Across-the-street. Ada and George were sitting in their chairs.

"What your ma say?" Ada asked.

211

"About what?"

"About you mowin' the lawn over this side."

"Ah, she didn't care," I lied.

"Back to school tomorrow, boy?" George said.

I nodded, thinking of Pal Pennick and wondering if I could learn to swim well enough.

"Soon be buyin' coal again," Ada sighed, looking out the window at the red woodbine leaves climbing the trunk of an elm. "Sixteen dollars a ton this year I hear," she said. "I don't know what they think folks is made of, money I guess."

Coal. Winter. Upstairs bedrooms cold as tombs. I didn't like to think of it. Summer was rushing to an end, faster every hour.

"How much coal does the bin hold?" I asked Ada. She looked at me funny, as if it was a strange question. "It ain't so much what the bin will hold, boy, it's how much folks can pay that matters."

"Did you ever hear of Red Feather Mines?" I asked. The question sounded like a poorly planned lie, but I had to get around to something.

"Heard of Red Feather *cee*-ment," said George. "It has a picture of a male cardinal on the front of the bag."

"No, not cement," I said. "Red Feather is a famous gold mine. My mother owns part of it and the stock went 'way up and we made a lot of extra money from it." What I was saying still sounded false, I thought, but maybe not to George and Ada. They didn't know anything about stocks, I knew that.

"Gold mine! My lands!" said Ada, looking at me as if I'd lost my senses.

"It's real," I said, taking the roll of money out of my pocket. "It really exists. Don't tell Mother, promise, but here's money for some coal."

I laid four ten dollar bills on top of the Stromberg-Carlson radio. "It's all right," I said, "it really did come from the gold mine."

The two of them just looked at the money. They needed it so much they couldn't touch it without fear.

"You won't tell, will you?" I said. "Please, just take it and buy the coal."

George laughed. "A gold mine's even better than a coal mine, I guess!" He was trying to make a joke, trying also to keep his good right hand from reaching out and taking the bills.

"Is it your ma's money?" Ada asked sternly.

"It's from the gold mine stock."

"You didn't steal it anyplace?"

"It's the same as if I *found* it somewhere," I said, trying to stay close to the truth.

Ada sniffed and walked into the kitchen. I knew she didn't believe me, but she didn't say anymore. I also knew she would pick up the $40 after I was gone.

I went out to George's garage and started the Chevy. The smell of the exhaust was sweet and the sound of the engine made the banty hens scurry around the yard. I backed the car out into the sun and let it sit with the engine running. The gas in the tank was almost gone.

If only it was true, I thought. If Red Feather Mines went up, Mother might buy a new car. She'd never buy the Airflow, but there was a 1936 Oldsmobile business coupe at Supple's she said she liked. She'd buy the Six, she said. It was black. The Eight cost almost a thousand dollars. Yet even the Six would be better than the Hudson.

The Red Sox were playing a holiday doubleheader with the Yankees. If it was June now instead of September, a doubleheader would be exciting, but the season was almost over and the Yanks were way ahead in the standings and it didn't matter much.

The piper came down the road before suppertime. As always, I was the only one who heard the reedy notes scrape through the evening air like the tired squeaks of old insects.

I went to meet him up the road, before he got to the hollow. I didn't want anyone to see us.

"You're still here, boy?" he said, seeing me sitting, waiting for him by the wall.

"You came back," I answered. I held my hand tight on what was left of the money.

"I won't be traveling when the cold comes," he said, letting the air exhale like a tired breath from the ragged bag. He came to the side of the road and let himself down onto the embankment where I sat.

"What else can you remember about my father?" I asked.

"You want to hear more?"

I nodded.

"Well, let's see, he was not a tall man, not big . . ."

"I know, but what was he *like*?"

"He had a way with him, a bearing. When he raised his gun to his shoulder and commanded me to *pull*! his size didn't matter. He was a master at what he was doing."

I could see him, smell the gunpowder, hear the shots. I had a box full of his spent shotgun shells I'd dug up just at the place where he had stood and called *pull*!

"Why did he stay here? In Hancock, I mean?"

"I couldn't say about that. I suppose he thought of it as home."

"He could have run away."

The piper chuckled at that. "Run away?"

214

A minute or two later the old man rose, shifting the weight of his bagpipes up onto his shoulder.

"Wait," I said. "Do people ever give you money?"

"I've earned money," he said. "Sometimes I play at weddings or funerals."

"If I give you something, would you say it was really from my father?"

"If you give me something, I wouldn't say anything, not even thank you."

"But why?"

"Because a boy would have nothing like that to give."

"But I *do*," I said, and held out what was left of Conductor Winter's money.

The piper looked at it, then at me. He opened his hand and took the bills as if we had both just found them lying by the side of the road. I didn't even know how much was left. I just wanted him to take it all.

"It's a lot of money for a man or a boy to *find*," he said, showing no emotion.

"It's yours—if you'll promise to always come back."

"It would buy me new pipes . . . if I didn't need it for other things." Then he put the money in his pocket as surely as if it had always been his.

"You will come back?"

He began filling the bag with air, his face puffing out and looking younger and happier as the wrinkles disappeared. Then the notes came again with the movement of his fingers and his feet began to keep cadence with the sound.

"It won't turn cold for quite a while," I said. "Will I see you again this year?"

"Perhaps, lad," he said, starting to move away from me with short, quick steps, like the beginning of a parade.

I didn't want to say goodbye, so I just waved.

He waved back without a pause in the music, then turned and marched off.

Summer went with him.